Author's Guide

ADDISON-WESLEY

An imprint of Addison Wesley Longman, Inc.

Reading, Massachusetts • Menlo Park, California • New York • Harlow, England
Don Mills, Ontario • Sydney • Mexico City • Madrid • Amsterdam

ISBN 0-201-36621-5

2 3 4 5 6 7 8 9 10 - VG - 01 00 99

Contents

Preface

Welcome to the Addison Wesley Longman (AWL) publishing companies—and specifically, to Addison-Wesley, our Reading, Massachusetts, hub. When you and Addison-Wesley conclude a publishing agreement, we become partners in a commercial and intellectual venture. The product of our partnership—whether a textbook, an on-line service, or a database of customizable course materials—will be a work into which you and we will have put a great deal of our time, money, energy, and ourselves. It will also be a product of teamwork, with success dependent on the diligence and good judgment of many individuals, including editors, marketers, design, production and manufacturing staff, and the sales force. Above all, it will involve you the author, for it is your vision and progress that determine the nature and pace of work of all the Addison-Wesley participants.

Successful partnerships are tight-knit relationships built on shared objectives, open communication, and a full understanding of mutual roles. To these ends, this *Addison-Wesley Author's Guide* lays out the stages of our publishing processes from manuscript preparation to revision planning. It introduces you to your publishing team and their respective roles, and it outlines the range of activities we will undertake on behalf of your work. It also addresses the specific support and information we will count on from you in order to publish and promote your work effectively. Each stage, as we hope you will see, is a matter of reciprocity, with the greater burden of responsibility and labor shifting from you at the outset to us at the end. All through the process, timing is essential to a successful result, and you will find frequent references to schedules in the following pages. We cannot state too emphatically that our prompt performance depends substantially on yours.

No guide, however helpful, can replace the close personal relationship between author and publisher. We will be in touch with you frequently throughout the publishing process. We are available to answer your questions and to help you solve any problems that arise.

We look forward to a satisfying and mutually beneficial partnership. Again, welcome.

ADDISON-WESLEY PUBLISHING TEAMS AND PROCESS OVERVIEW

Even though writing a textbook may seem a solitary process (there you are, alone with your word processor), there is nothing solitary about turning your ideas into a finished book. At Addison-Wesley we work in publishing teams that draw in different individuals and their competencies at different points in the product creation process. Following is an introduction to your publishing teams and to their roles in the publishing process.

PRESIGNING TEAM

The work that leads to a publishing agreement is of great importance to the ultimate success of the publishing enterprise because it sets out the common project goals (including the market and budget expectations) against which we will measure our progress and success. At the presigning stage we work hand in hand with you to shape your product vision and to flesh out the plans for the overall publishing process. You will meet and work directly with your acquisitions editor and other publishing professionals, including a development manager or development editor, a marketing manager, and a media/software producer.

ACQUISITIONS EDITOR

Acquisitions editors, also known as editors, are our eyes and ears on campus and our window into your discipline. On the go as much as they are in the office, our editors travel extensively to campuses around the country and to academic and professional conventions. Their goal is to keep up with emerging and developing trends and people in a given discipline. In many cases, the acquisitions editor will be the first Addison-Wesley staff member with whom you talk seriously about writing a book and is the individual with whom you will work most closely during the presigning stage and throughout the contract signing.

Your acquisitions editor will stay in regular touch with you while you are writing your book. (If you are a first-time author, this relationship will be invaluable.) He or she will advise you, for example, on the standard elements that should appear in the text (including pedagogical aids), the desired book length, and the number and types of illustrations you should include. You can also turn to your editor for advice on the content and organization of the chapters. During the writing stage, your editor will consult with a production supervisor or project editor who will later become your primary contact throughout the production cycle. We will talk more about the production supervisor's role in the next section.

Once you have drafted all or part of the manuscript, your acquisitions editor (or other editors; see below) will obtain **reviews** of your work. This involves sending the manuscript to instructors who teach the course in which your book will be used. The feedback your editor receives will help ensure that your text will be of high quality and will be well received in the market.

Your acquisitions editor's knowledge of the market is critical, both to you and to Addison-Wesley. It is the editor's responsibility to estimate the potential sales of the text and to establish a budget within which the text must be developed and produced. The editor must also determine what we need to do to make the book successful. For example, if every other book on the market has a comprehensive instructor's manual, yours must have one too.

Even after your final manuscript goes into production, your editor's involvement with your book continues. He or she works closely with the production department to make sure the book is published on time, and helps the marketing department plan the advertising and sales effort. Your editor will work with the marketing manager to present the book to the Addison-Wesley sales force at our national and regional sales meetings, and will follow up by talking with individual sales representatives. Throughout the publishing process, your acquisitions editor's contribution is critical to your book's ultimate success.

DEVELOPMENT EDITOR

In some cases, when the manuscript is aimed at a particularly large course (generally a required introductory-level course), a **development editor** may also be assigned to work with you and with the acquisitions editor. The development editor analyzes the nuts and bolts of your manuscript in order to compare your work with the most successful books in the field. The development editor's goal is the same as that of the acquisitions editor—to ensure that your book is of high quality and has the coverage and features it needs to be accepted in the market and to sell well. The development editor will also provide creative input, such as suggesting new pedagogical features and developing photo suggestions, text examples, and supplements.

When the first draft of the text is completed, it is time to develop the supporting visual program, and at this point the development editor will work closely with an **art editor**, who will set the vision for the art program and develop the color palette.

The development editor will also commission reviews and work with you to decide how to handle reviewers' comments, generally through a written analysis of the reviews, along with follow-up telephone conversations. You will appreciate the importance of this help when you are faced with sorting out the remarks of a dozen different reviewers, many of whom have slightly different views on the same material.

Your development editor will take a hands-on approach to your manuscript. You can expect her or him to work with you on organizational problems and to edit the manuscript for content, style, and level. Development editors also work closely with the design and production staff to make sure that the features you have worked on so diligently are presented properly; and they collaborate with marketing and sales to prepare advertising materials and information packets for the sales force.

MARKETING MANAGER

Our **marketing managers** provide the sales staff with the information needed to sell your book and help to prepare promotional material for potential adopters. This effort includes a comprehensive **marketing plan**, a targeted advertising campaign, marketing brochures, and presentations of the book at academic conventions and at our national sales meetings. Marketing managers work closely with the editorial and advertising department staffs, who write, design, and produce exciting promotional copy for brochures, catalogs, and the other components of the advertising campaign. Because our marketing managers specialize in a particular discipline, they have an intimate knowledge of the market and a wealth of ideas for marketing your text. In addition to the strategic marketing plan, they also offer valuable advice on the book's features and design, its cover, and the supplements program. The work of the marketing manager intensifies during the production cycle and continues after the text is published. During this critical time, you can expect to work closely with him or her (as well as with your acquisitions and development editors) to create accurate and effective sales tools. Once these marketing tools are complete, marketing managers turn their attention to the sales staff. During the main selling seasons, the marketing manager spends considerable time on campus, working directly with sales representatives to help sell your text and gather market feedback. The marketing manager continues to provide support and competitive market information as long as the book is being sold.

MEDIA/SOFTWARE PRODUCER

As instructors increasingly rely on digital technologies, the need has arisen to provide specialized new media supplements and services to our markets. At Addison-Wesley, highly skilled **media/software producers** are responsible for the development of all digital media products to accompany our textbooks, including videos, laser discs, and CD-ROMs, as well as software to support individual textbooks or disciplines. Your media/software producer may work with you in the presigning stage to ensure that the team is aware of all multiple media delivery options and to help plan the media production process.

CORE PUBLISHING TEAM

The primary role of the **Core Publishing Team** is to implement the authorial and editorial vision of the project and to share responsibility for its budgetary goals. Team members include the Presigning Team and a project editor, an associate or assistant editor, or an editorial assistant; plus a production supervisor.

PROJECT MANAGER, ASSOCIATE EDITOR, AND ASSISTANT EDITOR

A **project manager**, **associate editor**, or **assistant editor** from the editorial staff may be assigned to work with you in the development stages of your book. These editors will assist you by coordinating such tasks as sending your manuscript out for review and summarizing the reviewers' feedback, monitoring the overall schedule and budget, and preparing your text and art manuscripts for transmittal to production. They may also work with you in shaping the supplements program that may be planned for your book.

EDITORIAL ASSISTANT

An **editorial assistant** is available to you throughout the publishing process and may be in charge of such editorial matters such as sending manuscript out for review, assembling reviews as they come in, and providing summary information. The editorial assistant reports directly to the acquisitions editor and is therefore able to alert the editor to any situation that might require his or her immediate attention.

PRODUCTION SUPERVISOR (PROJECT EDITOR)

The process of turning your words, photographs, and illustration sketches into a book is handled by the Addison-Wesley production team, which is made up of production supervisors, designers, art editors, production technology specialists, and manufacturing specialists.

Each manuscript is assigned to a **production supervisor (project editor)**, who oversees the production process and maintains close contact with you and with your acquisitions and development editors while your book is in production. It is the production supervisor's job to keep your book on schedule and to oversee the entire production cycle, including copyediting of the text manuscript, all proof stages, and coordination of the art program. We will consider the responsibilities of the production supervisor further in Chapter 10.

Your production supervisor works with designers and art editors to develop the aesthetic appeal of the book. Although the length of the book and the size of each page (known as the **trim size**) have already been determined, no decisions have yet been made on page design. Working with guidelines provided by the editors and the production supervisor, the **designer** makes decisions about the many factors that define the book's appearance, such as typefaces, chapter opener layout, and the style for tables, boxed text, and end-of-chapter material.

The production supervisor also works with the prepress/media buyer, who is responsible for the quality control of the electronic book files and in turn works with the compositor and printer to make sure that the overall production schedule is met.

EXTENDED PUBLISHING TEAM

The primary role of the **Extended Publishing Team** is to offer guidance and input during the early stages of product planning and to implement all aspects of the production plan. The Extended Publishing Team includes the Core Publishing Team members and a number of highly skilled specialists who move in and out of the production process as needed.

ART EDITOR

Consulting with the other team members, the art editor creates and styles the illustration program. For revised editions with art styles in place, and for books with minimal art programs, a freelance art editor may be hired to prepare the art manuscript and track the proofing stages.

DESIGNER

The designer works with the team to create a distinctive interior text design and cover design that reflect market needs and customer expectations. A consultant on the art program as well, the designer plays a crucial role in translating the author's vision into a physical book.

PREPRESS/MEDIA BUYER

The **prepress/media buyer** collaborates with others to ensure high-quality typesetting and page design, to test electronic files, and to select appropriate outside suppliers for essential services.

TECHNICAL ART SUPERVISOR

The **technical art supervisor** works with the team to evaluate files from art vendors and/or authors and advises authors on file preparation.

CREATIVE SERVICES MANAGER

The **creative services manager** works with the team to design and develop the marketing and advertising materials. These items include everything from postcards and brochures to elaborate convention displays, as well as comprehensive catalogs of our print and electronic products.

SUPPLEMENTS EDITOR

It is a powerful trend in college publishing markets today that professors adopt teaching "systems" rather than just a textbook. The quality of the **supplements** (instructor's manual, test bank, study guide, computerized test bank, PowerPoint presentations, and so forth) is thus an important factor in the textbook adoption decision. Because we recognize this reality, we will assign you either a **supplements editor** or a book team member dedicated to the supplements package to coordinate the development and production of the ancillaries for your book. Whether you produce your own supplements or others are hired to do so, these individuals will be crucial in ensuring your book's eventual success.

PERMISSIONS EDITOR

Part of your writing responsibilities includes obtaining all necessary **permissions** to reprint material taken from other sources. Detailed information on obtaining permissions is covered in Chapter 5. However, if any questions or problems should arise during this process, a **permissions editor** is available to help you address them.

REPRINT AND ARCHIVE COORDINATOR

No matter how careful we all are, minor errors can creep into a text–typos that should have been caught, missing cross-references, misplaced illustration labels, and so on. The **reprint and archive coordinator** maintains a file of these errors and makes sure they are corrected when the book is reprinted (see Chapter 10). It is very important that your reprint corrections be on file with your acquisitions editor as soon as possible after the book is published, so that when the reprint order comes from manufacturing they can be incorporated into the new printing.

SALES STAFF

With a marketing and selling network that spans the world, Addison Wesley Longman has one of the largest sales forces in the industry. Given their size and reach, our sales staff are able to sample and sell your book to virtually all potential customers.

CAMPUS SALES REPRESENTATIVES

We maintain a staff of over 175 sales representatives, operating from three regional offices. Each **sales representative** travels throughout a particular area of the country, known as a territory, visiting schools in that area and calling regularly on instructors of all courses for which we publish texts.

Sales representatives must master an enormous amount of information about courses and about the Addison-Wesley texts that are appropriate for them. They must also know the strengths and weaknesses of competing books. Thus, a knowledgeable sales representative can discuss your text effectively with individual instructors and can answer any questions about the book, the course, and the competition.

Our representatives take care of all of the details that may mean the difference between making and losing a sale. They check that **complimentary copies** of the text, known as sample copies, are sent to instructors. If book adoptions are decided by committee, the sales representatives make sure that all committee members have seen the book and the sales materials describing it. Most of all, during this entire process, they are available for customers' questions; and if they are unsure of an answer, they have the resources of the Addison-Wesley marketing department to back them up.

Even after an adoption, our representatives offer continuing service to instructors. They make sure that books and supplements reach campus on time for the new semester. When instructors begin using the text, they follow through to check that all course needs have been met.

Our sales representatives give us an enormous amount of grassroots-level feedback on our books. Because they are in constant touch with instructors, they learn how effective our books are in actual classroom use. They communicate what they learn to the acquisitions editor, who in turn passes it on to authors preparing revisions. Sales representatives also work with editors to find potential reviewers for subsequent editions (the most attractive candidates are instructors who have insight into a book's strengths and weaknesses; we discuss the review process in Chapter 3).

Sales representatives are often the first to perceive a hole in the market–the need for a fresh and innovative text. And, just as important, they often find instructors with the credentials and experience to write such a book. Our acquisitions editors thus listen carefully to advice from sales representatives, our closest link to a rapidly changing market.

TELESALES REPRESENTATIVES AND SALES ASSISTANTS

In contrast to sales representatives who visit instructors on campus, our **telesales representatives** use the telephone to make sales calls. Because it is virtually impossible for our sales representatives to go to every school in their territories, the telesales representatives fill the gap. Instructors in small schools in particular receive a great deal of individual attention from our telesales staff. Telesales representatives have many of the same responsibilities as sales representatives—describing Addison-Wesley books to potential adopters, sending out desk copies, and closing sales.

To support the needs of professors, we also have a staff of sales assistants, whose sole responsibility is to provide access to and information about Addison-Wesley textbooks. Among the specific services that professors can obtain by calling a toll-free number is access to desk copies and to information about textbooks and supplements, including changes of editions. Because of our commitment to service, the regional office structure has become an integral part of Addison-Wesley's marketing strategy.

THE INTERNATIONAL PUBLISHING GROUP

Addison Wesley Longman sells its texts not only in the United States but throughout the world. The **International Publishing Group** has staff in many countries to serve its authors and customers.

The International Publishing Group consists of seven regional companies that publish and distribute textbooks in local and regional markets. Publishing activity encompasses preschool to college-level materials in local languages and in English. Higher education titles are distributed as published by the two main originating units—U.S and U.K Higher Education, and CEPUB—in lower-cost World Student Series (WSS) and International Student Editions (ISE).

Local-language higher education publishing exists in Latin America, Spain, Korea, Taiwan, and Japan. Copublishing operations flourish in Korea, Taiwan, and Japan. Addision Wesley Longman U.S. and U.K. titles are translated for overseas higher education markets.

The goal of the International Publishing Group is to extend Addison Wesley Longman's main U.S. and U.K. copyrights into world markets and to develop local publishing opportunities in markets that will support the effort and that have the editorial and sales infrastructure to develop the market fully.

OTHER SALES CHANNELS

The Higher Education Publishing Group at Addison-Wesley also has a variety of sales organizations that market and sell college titles in nonacademic markets. These markets include business, industry, professional, and government accounts; conventions; mail-order customers; specialty distribution; retail accounts; wholesalers; and book clubs. We sell to these markets through telesales, direct mail, journal advertising, convention attendance, and special programs and workshops. Your editor and marketing manager will work closely and aggressively with their counterparts in these special sales channels to promote your book to nonacademic markets.

BOOKSELLER RELATIONS PROGRAM

Addison Wesley Longman has implemented a **Bookseller Relations Program** to address the specific issues brought up by bookstores. The mission of this program is to provide excellent and distinctive service to our customers and to foster an environment conducive to developing outstanding partnerships with our retailers, through vendor/retailer partnerships that emphasize cooperation rather than competition. We are always evaluating changing needs within the industry and looking for new ways to improve service to our customers.

CUSTOM BOOK MANAGER

The Higher Education Publishing Group includes Addison Wesley Longman *Custom Publishing,* an operation created to meet the diverse needs of a changing marketplace. The goal of the **custom book manager** is to set the standard for quality and service in custom publishing and in the alternative delivery of educational materials to customers. Addison Wesley Longman Custom Publishing makes your book more competitive in the marketplace by allowing potential adopters to select from it material based on the particular content and approach they prefer for their courses.

Custom book managers work closely with sales, editorial, and marketing personnel to adapt textbooks to the special needs of a professor, school, or association and to sell the finished products. They not only coordinate the publishing process for these projects but also continually look for additional opportunities to market your book to new audiences.

DEVELOPING THE BOOK PLAN

In some sense, the easiest part of your work begins when you start writing your manuscript. By then, you have a clear idea of where you are going and how you are going to get there. To reach this stage, you have to go through what might best be described as a birth process: You have to create a book plan. It is no exaggeration to say that this plan will determine the success of your project. It will define your book, its supplements, and the work you must do to write them. Your Addison-Wesley team will work with you throughout this stage to ensure that your book and package will meet the needs of the market. The following steps will help you to develop your book plan.

STEP 1: KNOW YOUR AUDIENCE

You cannot begin to plan without knowing your book's audience—the instructors and students who will use your book in the classroom. Always keep in mind that your book must appeal to these two distinct groups, but that in the end, the needs of instructors to teach and students to learn coincide.

When sales representatives hand out a complimentary copy of your book to instructors, the instructors know fairly quickly whether the book meets their needs. They look for a table of contents covering all the topics taught in their course, but the inclusion of the most up-to-date research findings or a fair presentation of conflicting points of view might be other key considerations. They may also analyze the supplements program to be sure that it contains the desired elements.

In addition, the instructors assess the level and pacing of the material. Uppermost in their minds is whether the book is appropriate for their particular students. If, for example, they are teaching an introductory-level course at a quarter school, they need a straightforward, fairly simple presentation that covers the material but does not overwhelm readers with detail. If, on the other hand, they are teaching the same course at a semester school, they might assume that the students can handle much more depth and detail.

Even instructors who are convinced that a book is right for their courses will quickly change their minds if their students have trouble with it. Students must be able to use your text to master the subject matter. If your book is filled with esoteric references that students cannot understand or with jargon appropriate to a scholarly journal, students will not learn. Similarly, if the book does not take students down a clear path from point A to point B, or if it assumes that readers have the background to draw their own conclusions about material they are learning for the first time, it will fall short as a teaching tool.

Always remember that your book will sell only if it succeeds in the classroom and meets the needs of students and teachers. Thus, a critical part of the planning process involves finding out exactly who your audience is and how best to communicate with them. Begin by looking at the best-selling books for the course. Analyze what needs are currently being met by existing books, and determine to match or better them. Next, analyze what needs are not currently being met, and develop innovative solutions to address those needs.

STEP 2: DEVELOP YOUR TABLE OF CONTENTS

This step involves nothing less than organizing your whole project. You must decide, right at the start, how to separate the body of knowledge that is the subject of your book into distinct parts and chapters. It is important to remember at this point that you do not have to reinvent the wheel. By talking to your acquisitions editor about how a range of instructors teaches the course, by analyzing competing texts, and by looking back at your own classroom experience, you will be able to develop a workable table of contents.

We are not implying that you should stop here. On the contrary, it is at this point that your creative juices should start to flow. Use this information as a springboard for what may be an even *more* effective way of organizing the text. If, after talking to people, you realize that students have a hard time understanding one section of the course, consider adding another chapter to clarify the material. Or if you find out that a chapter included in every existing text is rarely covered in the course, consider eliminating it to give yourself more space for what is really important.

Go through this same discovery process to organize the material in each chapter. Then create detailed outlines that show all of the headings that will appear in the chapters. In most cases, it is best to stick with three heading levels. For example, if you are writing a chapter in a business text on "Producing Products and Services," one of your discussions might be organized in the following way:

I. Facility Location
    A. What Constitutes a Good Location?
        1. Proximity to raw materials
        2. Proximity to markets
        3. Availability of personnel
        4. Transportation

Of course, how much you can write on any given topic is limited by the total number of pages in the book. This figure will be given to you by your acquisitions editor. For ease of classroom use, books for some courses—for example, many business and economics courses—should have chapters that are all approximately the same length. If your outline shows that you have to cover too much in one chapter, consider breaking the material into two chapters. Chapter 6 of this *Author's Guide* gives you the tools you will need to estimate the length of your manuscript. Always remember that your goal in deciding chapter length and organization is to make the material as accessible as possible, without sacrificing coverage or quality.

STEP 3: DEFINE THE PEDAGOGICAL ELEMENTS OF THE TEXT

Pedagogical elements are learning tools—devices that make it easier for students to understand and apply chapter content. The particular elements you choose will be influenced by your book's level and subject matter (an introductory-level business text is more likely to include boxed case studies than an advanced calculus text, for example) and by what the competition offers (for instance, if every other text includes case studies, this is probably a clear signal that case studies are important to customers). When used effectively, pedagogical elements give you a way of making the text more interesting. For example, by adding boxed case studies that apply academic concepts to current or everyday situations, you are relating the material to students' knowledge base, hooking them into the discussion, and helping them learn.

TYPICAL PEDAGOGICAL ELEMENTS

The pedagogical elements used in many texts include the following:

    Learning Objectives. Learning objectives preview the major concepts of the chapter and can be presented in narrative or list form. They give students an idea of what they will learn and in what order.

Boxed Essays. Boxed essays, or **boxes**, apply academic concepts to real life or provide additional examples to clarify complex topics. They also have an important visual effect on the text. By breaking up long discussions, they help students digest the material in the chapter. The danger in using this device is that students often think that anything set off from the main text does not have to be read or learned. Therefore, be wary of presenting important concepts in a box unless they are thoroughly covered in the text itself. And do not rely on boxes to communicate the chapter theme. (See Chapter 4 for additional information on boxes.)

Key Terms. Every academic field has its own vocabulary—terms that enable experts to talk to one another readily. Students must be introduced in a systematic way to the **key terms** that define your field. These definitions must build on one another to form a solid foundation for future learning. Thus, you should define all key terms the first time they are used (and distinguish them with boldface type) and perhaps include a list of these terms at the end of each chapter. Many texts include important terms and their definitions in an end-of-text glossary (see Chapter 8).

Marginal Notes. Marginal notes present key concepts or terms in the margin of a single-column text. They are more likely to appear in introductory-level texts.

Case Studies. Case studies apply academic concepts to real-world examples. They are frequently used in business, economics, finance, psychology, and sociology texts, among others.

Summaries. Summaries help students learn the material in a chapter by recapping and reinforcing critical concepts in narrative or list form. They assist students in focusing on the essential content within the chapter. Summaries may occur at the end of major sections and/or at the end of a chapter.

Review Questions. Review questions generally fall at the end of each chapter and test students' knowledge of what they have read. They also refocus the material and help students look at it in a slightly different way.

Additional Readings. Many texts end each chapter with a list of books and articles on chapter topics. **Annotated bibliographies**, which give a short description of each entry's contents, can be especially helpful. Alternatively, the additional readings can appear at the end of the text, preferably listed by chapter.

OTHER PEDAGOGICAL AIDS

Depending on the subject matter of your book, it may be useful to include **part openers**, which introduce each part of the text and may contain outlines of the chapters included in the part and a brief text introduction to the part; and/or **chapter outlines**, which list the main chapter headings. In an introductory or intermediate economics textbook, **sample problems and solutions** that show students how to approach and solve typical problems might also be attractive to the market. Your acquisitions and development editors will help you decide which elements are appropriate for your text.

STEP 4: CREATE YOUR ILLUSTRATION PROGRAM

A picture really is worth a thousand words. The **line art** (charts, graphs, and diagrams that are drawn by an art studio), photographs, cartoons, maps, and **camera-ready art** (line art ready to be photographed as supplied, without redrawing) that you choose to illustrate each chapter are often as important as the words on the page. So never treat them as an afterthought or as someone else's responsibility, for they are critical to your book's success. Discuss with your editors the number of illustrations of each type that are appropriate for the text. Then calculate the average number of illustrations for each chapter, and use this number as a guideline while you write.

Let the subject matter guide your choice of illustrations. Remember that the objective of each illustration is to help students learn the material—to give them a visual way of approaching concepts that have already been explained in words. To be effective, each illustration must be closely integrated with the text. In most cases, the text will describe the concept, and the illustration will reinforce the description. A caption is then added to reinforce the concept once more.

The success of your illustration program depends on your ability to think visually. Try to integrate your verbal and visual presentations by jotting down ideas for line art and photographs while you are drafting the text. You will be surprised at how quickly your list of suggestions grows. As always, it is important to know what the competition offers, so review their illustration programs carefully. Then you will be better able to create a superior program for your own book. (See Chapter 9 for detailed information on preparing illustrations.)

STEP 5: PLAN THE FRONT AND BACK OF THE TEXT

Front matter and back matter are more than a wrapping for the "meat" of your text. On the contrary, they contain important learning and marketing tools. Usually included in the **front matter** are the table of contents and the preface, which set the tone for the book and tell potential adopters exactly what will be covered. The **back matter** typically comprises one or more appendixes, a glossary, reference lists, and one or more indexes. In addition, you should determine whether to include any material on the front endpapers and back endpapers, such as lists of symbols used in the text or lists of a particular type of box. It is important to talk with your editors early in the planning stage to decide which elements to include and what to consider when writing them. (See Chapter 8 for a more complete discussion of front and back matter.)

STEP 6: PLAN THE SUPPLEMENTS

At the same time that you plan your text, you must also consider the text **supplements**—the free and salable materials that are a part of the text "package." You and your acquisitions editor will determine the requirements of the market, which vary widely. Whereas texts for some advanced courses have no supplements, packages for large-enrollment introductory courses can be substantial.

Supplements are extremely important marketing tools and often are crucial factors in instructors' adoption decisions. Savvy instructors compare the packages of competing texts to find the most complete, effective set of supplementary resources. Because your book will be judged not as a text alone but as a text accompanied by supporting materials, never view the time that you spend planning the supplements as a distraction from more important work. To instructors in many disciplines, supplements are as important as the text itself.

Among the most popular supplements are instructor's manuals, study guides, transparencies, test banks, laboratory manuals, answer keys, and solutions manuals—in either print or electronic form. In many markets, software, videos, or multimedia may be important components of the learning package. And World Wide Web sites offering such resources as text updates, student self-tests, and links to other sites are increasingly common. Because many of these elements are expensive to produce, the market must be large enough to support them, especially if they are provided without charge.

The bigger the supplements package, the earlier the planning must start; in many cases, you must enlist the help of qualified support authors to work on various projects. Always remember that although you may turn over work to other authors, ultimately you will be judged by the content and quality of your supplements program. (For a more detailed discussion of supplements packages, see Chapter 11.)

STEP 7: CREATE A SCHEDULE

Authors live by the word—and by the schedule. From the moment you sign a contract, you will be forced to think about the development and production schedules for your book and supplements package. You will have to give us a manuscript by a specified date if we are to publish your book in time for major adoptions and in the best competitive position. It is important that you assess your workload realistically, and to do so means being honest with yourself about how you will schedule your writing around your teaching and research responsibilities and how much time the writing will actually take. It is vital to your project's success that you keep to the schedule set right at the beginning.

Many authors who write the first draft on time fall into the trap of scheduling too little time for the necessary tasks of revision and rewriting. This work can be extremely time-consuming, especially if reviewers or editors suggest substantial changes. Although no one looks forward to reorganizing a chapter or adding or deleting material, you can be sure that your work will result in a higher-quality product with greater appeal to the intended audience.

You must also set aside time to work on your book as it goes through production. As you will see in Chapter 10, you will review the copyedited manuscript and illustration proofs, as well as proofread typeset copy in at least one proof stage. Depending on the complexity of your project, production of the text alone will probably take between 6 and 12 months; and the supplements require additional time as well. The key to successful scheduling is an open line of communication with your editors. If you run into scheduling problems, we will do everything we can to help.

Reviewing Your Proposal and Manuscript

Ask any Broadway actor or Hollywood star what he or she thinks of reviews. The response will likely be "I hate them—unless, of course, they're good!" The knowledge that no one likes reviews should ease your discomfort when it is time to see what other academic experts think of your work. Recognizing that the review process is difficult at best will help make the experience a lot easier. The most important thing to remember is that reviews are intended to help us publish the best book we can.

Stages in the Reviewing Process

The **reviewing process** takes place in stages, from the time of the initial proposal through the publication of the finished text. (See Chapter 13 for information on how this process differs for revisions.)

REVIEWING THE INITIAL PROPOSAL

Your acquisitions editor will send your initial proposal—prospectus, table of contents, and sample chapters—out for review to determine whether the idea of the book and your writing style fit the needs of the market. At this stage, reviewers are asked for opinions on text organization, the completeness of the table of contents, the general approach, and how the sample chapters compare with corresponding chapters in texts they are currently using.

REVIEWING THE FIRST-DRAFT MANUSCRIPT

In the planning stage, your editors will work with you to determine the type of reviewing necessary to ensure the success of your project. The first-draft manuscript is often reviewed in stages to provide the author with early feedback. (This process may be specified in your contract.) The first-draft manuscript is sent to experts in the field and professors teaching the course to assess the scope, accu-racy, clarity, and marketability of the manuscript. The total number of reviews varies from two or three critiques by subject experts for advanced or highly specialized works to dozens of content, pedagogical, and marketing reviews for large-market introductory texts.

REVIEWING THE REVISED AND FINAL-DRAFT MANUSCRIPT

Assuming that your initial reviews are generally favorable, your editors will commission another set of reviews for the revised manuscript. Although this may turn out to be the final round, it is more likely that you will need to make changes to the revised draft before final reviews are undertaken. Your manuscript will not be accepted for production until the final reviews have been evaluated by your editors. The key question reviewers are asked at this stage is, "Would you adopt this text for use in your course?"

POST-PUBLICATION REVIEWS

Following publication, your marketing manager may decide to commission one or more reviews comparing your text with its principal competitors. These **post-publication reviews** are usually obtained from faculty who are currently using the competing texts. Comparative reviews at this stage give your editors and marketing manager the information they need to execute the sales strategy for your book.

WHO REVIEWS YOUR BOOK?

Reviewers are chosen by your acquisitions editor or development editor from a pool of qualified candidates he or she knows and from recommendations made by Addison Wesley Longman sales representatives. A reviewer's most important qualifications are experience in teaching the course, use of a previous edition of your text or one of the competing books, and a sound knowledge of the field. We are always looking for qualified reviewers to help evaluate new projects—including yours—and welcome any suggestions you may have. If there are any instructors in your field whose opinions you value, your editor will consider giving them the opportunity to evaluate your work. Although we will tell you the schools at which the reviewers teach so that you can evaluate, for example, how well your manuscript is being received at a four-year school versus a community college, you will not usually be made aware of the identity of the reviewers until you see their names in the acknowledgments section of the preface. With the exception of revisions of widely used texts, they will not typically know who you are.

Writing and Developing the Manuscript

Addison-Wesley chooses its authors because of their unique professional backgrounds, teaching experience, and knowledge of the course and competing texts. We come to you because we believe in your ability to write a text that will find a place in the market. Although this *Author's Guide* cannot tell you how to write a textbook (no one can do that), we believe that we can help you along in the process by setting certain standards for tone, consistency, and style. Our goal is to remove any barriers that stand in the way of your direct communication with students.

Talk Directly to Students

Professional writers have an old trick that lets them know if they are talking directly to their audience. They read their manuscript out loud to see if their tone is simple and direct. Even if you are a first-time author, you can strive for the same effect. By being helpful rather than distant, conversational rather than lecturelike, straightforward rather than convoluted, you can make your text enjoyable and easy to read. And you should strive for a pace that enables students to assimilate the material without becoming confused or bogged down in detail. Always remember that learning new material is tough enough without unclear language and a confusing presentation getting in the way.

Use Accepted Standards of Style

Stylistic inconsistencies hinder good communication. Even if they are not aware of it, readers are most comfortable when the same styling rules apply throughout a text. Thus, we urge our authors to follow the spelling standards outlined in *Webster's New Collegiate Dictionary* and the styling standards set forth in the latest edition of *The Chicago Manual of Style*, published by the University of Chicago Press. The latter volume, which is known universally as *The Chicago Manual*, or simply *Chicago*, is the "Bible" in matters of punctuation, abbreviations, capitalization, footnote and bibliographic style, and format. Although our copyeditors will edit your manuscript according to *Chicago* rules, you will save yourself—and us—a great deal of time and work if you apply these standards at the start. You will also reduce the possibility of confusion and mistakes, for whenever we change your language we run the risk of misinterpretation.

There are times, of course, when *The Chicago Manual* will not apply. Many academic disciplines have their own professional guidelines that supersede *Chicago* style. For example, special rules may apply to the use of abbreviations, units of measure, footnote and bibliographic style, and capitalization. If this is the case, inform your editors at the start that you are following a different style and tell them how it differs.

It is important to develop a system for keeping track of all of the styling decisions you make. While writing, keep a list, or **style sheet**, of how you choose (there's often a choice) to spell technical terms and of how to treat capitalizations, abbreviations, and so on. Be sure to follow the same rules throughout your manuscript and to give the style sheet to us along with your first draft. You will also receive a style sheet prepared by the copyeditor later on.

AVOID SEXIST LANGUAGE AND ETHNIC STEREOTYPES

For years, **sexist language** was a part of every textbook. This language was not a matter of conscious discrimination but just the "way things were done." We at Addison-Wesley, and indeed the whole publishing field, have come a long way since then. Sexist language, even when used inadvertently, is no longer acceptable; and we do our best to weed it out of every manuscript we publish.

We encourage our authors to start this weeding-out process by avoiding sexist language in the first place. Do not assume that your readers are exclusively male by using only "he" as a personal pronoun. Alternatives include using the phrase "he or she" and providing a mix of examples, some featuring a female and others featuring a male. Another way to eliminate sexist language is to recast passages in the plural—a task that may take a little thought at first but soon will come naturally. Your text should also reflect the wide ethnic diversity of your audience, in both writing and illustrative material (text examples, photographs, and the like).

USE A CONSISTENT FORMAT

A consistent format helps put readers at ease, for they know what to expect from chapter to chapter. You must decide in advance how to style elements such as headings, tables, boxes, captions, and lists. As we will suggest in greater detail in Chapter 7, it is important for you to start thinking in terms of consistency of format from the moment that you sit down to prepare the first draft. Although the consistent preparation of your manuscript is most important in the final draft, the first draft should also be as clear as possible; the better prepared the manuscript, the better the reviewers will respond to it. Remember that the elements we are about to discuss are just a few examples of elements that may be included in your book.

HEADINGS

Headings are useful because they help to organize the material and divide it into digestible chunks. But they can be confusing if they are not used consistently. Thus, before you start writing, you must answer these questions:

1. How many main headings, on average, should I use in each chapter?
2. How many subheading levels are appropriate? (In most books, there should be no more than three levels of heading.)
3. How should I construct the headings? (One should not, for example, alternate phrases with full sentences.)

TABLES

Tables communicate difficult or complicated concepts in a shorthand way. Their goal is to explain and simplify material, not make it harder to learn. Thus, you should avoid putting too much information in tables and instead create a greater number of smaller tables that are easy to understand. However, it is important not to make a table so simple that it is a waste of space; the general rule is to include the information in whatever format takes up the least space. If you can cover the topic in a sentence or less, it is probably not appropriate to include it in tabular form unless the material requires special emphasis. Aim also for consistency in table headings. If your column headings are all capitals in one table, they should be all capitals in all tables. And use the same table construction style throughout.

GRAPHS, FLOW CHARTS, AND OTHER VISUALS

Material that is presented in a table often can be more easily comprehended in another format. Precise empirical data may need to be in tabular format, but be open to enlivening your presentation by thinking of alternative formats, such as graphs, flow charts, and time lines, that make concepts easier to grasp.

BOXED ESSAYS

Boxed essays, or boxes, contain chapter material set off from the main text. Decide at the start what you want your boxed essays to accomplish. Some authors use them to present the latest—and most controversial—research findings, whereas others include material relevant to students' own lives. The boxes may feature profiles of famous people in their disciplines or present interesting real-world applications. In some disciplines, the summary material appears in boxes, and in others, such as English handbooks, rules may be set off in this way. Decide on the number of boxes you want to include in each chapter and try to stick with this number throughout the text. As you can imagine, it is disconcerting for students to find six boxes in one chapter and only one box in all of the remaining chapters; their importance and applicability to the text material becomes unclear. Also determine what format and length the boxes should be and what number and kinds of illustrations you will use, and then apply these decisions consistently.

CAPTIONS

Captions are brief descriptions that accompany illustrations. In the past, they were referred to as *legends*, but this term currently applies only to explanatory material related to maps. Strive to include the same level of information in all of the captions; that is, aim for a consistent level of detail. For example, if you were writing an economics text, it would be poor form to have one photo caption read, "Hundreds of millions of shares of stock are traded each day on the New York Stock Exchange. On October 19, 1987, the day of the market crash, a record number of 604,330,410 shares were traded," while the caption under a facing photo reads, "A market specialist." Although some disciplines may require more detail, as a general rule try to hold your caption length to no more than two sentences. *Never* present new material in a caption. A caption should reiterate what has already been said in the text, and the text should refer students to the illustration for further clarification.

LISTS

Lists make it easy for students to pick out important material. But once again, students can be distracted if the format of the list gets in the way. Do not mix full sentences and phrases within a list, and do not use numbered lists in one place and lettered lists in another. Also, the numbering loses its usefulness if the elements become so long that the list extends more than a page or two. In general, once you have decided on a style and format, use it consistently from list to list.

WORKING WITH COAUTHORS

If you are writing a text along with one or more **coauthors**, it is important that you work together to achieve a consistent result. Here are suggestions for working with coauthors:

1. Agree in advance on a detailed table of contents. The table of contents can change and evolve during the development process, but you should have a clear understanding among yourselves of the scope of the book and what each author will cover.

2. Agree in advance on issues of style and format. Create a style sheet that will guide everyone's work. It is important that from the earliest stages you agree on what features you will include, what you will title them, how many you will include, and so on.

3. Exchange chapters on a regular basis. Read and critique each other's material carefully to be sure that the writing has the same tone, style, degree of detail, and conceptual complexity.

4. Discuss reviews together, and be sure you are of one mind as to the thrust of what the reviewers are saying and how you will revise the manuscript in response to the reviews.

5. Remain in close contact throughout the manuscript development process. Whether through regular e-mail exchanges, faxes, conference calls, or in-person meetings, commit to working together. Keep your coauthor informed of changes in your thinking. For example, if you see that you must unexpectedly cover a particular topic in a chapter that you are working on, let your coauthor know in order to avoid duplicating each other's work.

WORKING WITH A COORDINATING AUTHOR

Coordinating authors have an extremely important role in the book's development. They tie together the pieces of the book through their writing of the introduction and part openers and make sure that all of the contributors know exactly what they must do. Coordinating authors work with editors to decide on the final table of contents, and help contributors determine the length of each chapter and chapter due dates. They also read all drafts before they are sent to the editors and work with the editors to decide how to handle reviewers' comments. Most important, coordinating authors are the final arbiters in disputes about text content and style, and they are responsible for submitting the manuscript on time.

OBTAINING PERMISSIONS

Your writing responsibilities include obtaining all necessary **permissions** to reprint materials taken from other sources. The best time to begin applying for permissions is while you are researching and writing the manuscript. If you wait too long and permission is denied, you will have to delete the copy or find a suitable substitute and rewrite the accompanying text as necessary. Or you may decide not to use the material because the permission fee is too high. In any case, delays in requesting permissions could result in delays in the schedule of your book.

A request for permission is not, in most instances, a commitment to use the material; however, if you change your mind after permission has been granted, you should inform the copyright holder that the material will not be used. Some permission sources set a deadline for canceling—beyond this date you may be responsible for all of, or a portion of, the fee even if the material is not used. Permission fees are customarily paid upon publication, but be sure to read the small print in each letter for exceptions. Some publishers and agents now request payment prior to publication, often within 30 to 90 days of the request. In such cases, decide whether you really want to use the material involved because few sources will refund a fee on a prepaid permission. Addison-Wesley will pay any fees and charge them as specified in your contract. Upon publication, we will also send complimentary copies of your book to copyright holders when required by the permission contract.

COPYRIGHT LAW

A **copyright** is the exclusive legal right to reproduce, publish, and sell a literary, dramatic, musical, or artistic work. The law grants to the owner of the copyright for the work the exclusive rights to do and to authorize any of the following:

1. To reproduce the copyrighted work
2. To prepare derivative works
3. To distribute copies of the copyrighted work to the public by sale, rental, lease, or lending
4. In certain cases, such as for literary and musical works, to perform the copyrighted work publicly
5. In certain cases, such as for graphics, images, or other audiovisuals, to display the copyrighted work publicly

Written permission must be obtained to use all copyrighted material. Works published prior to January 1, 1978, are protected for 75 years. (See *The Chicago Manual* for details concerning this material.) Works published on or after January 1, 1978, are copyrighted for the life of the author, plus 50 years. A work made for hire (such as an instructor's manual) is copyrighted for 75 years from publication or 100 years from creation, whichever is shorter.

Public domain refers to material on which copyright has expired or material that, owing to its nature, is not protected by copyright. Most government publications, as well as commonplace information such as height and weight charts, are considered to be in the public domain. Works published in the United States 75 years prior to the current year are in the public domain. However, a new translation or new version of a work in the public domain can be protected by copyright; if you are not sure of whether something is in the public domain, the safest course is to request permission.

WHEN DO YOU NEED PERMISSION?

Any material in your book that is borrowed from another source (including other Addison-Wesley books and even material from friends and relatives) may require written permission. The goal is to distinguish between material that can be used without obtaining permission (see the section on "Fair Use," below) and material for which permission is necessary. These guidelines should help you decide the majority of cases; when in doubt, please consult the permissions editor.

1. Quoted material from books, articles, Web sites, the Internet, and so on: Any quoting (whether one long quote or several shorter quotes from the same source) requires permission from the copyright holder unless it is determined to be fair use (see the "Fair Use" section).

2. Poems, plays, songs: You need to get permission for any quote from a poem, play, or song, regardless of length.

3. Photographs and artwork (including cartoons): All require permission from the copyright holder. Sometimes rights are controlled by a photo agency, a cartoon syndicate, or the magazine in which the illustration appears. Sometimes the artist holds the copyright. You may be required to estimate the portion of the book page that the illustration will fill (full page, ½ page, ¼ page, and so on). In rare cases, photographs or artwork may be in the public domain (that is, no one holds rights to them). Please don't make this assumption without checking with the source or with us.

4. Figures, graphs, charts, tables, tests, quizzes: These require permission. Figures are often changed by redrawing. The term "redrawing" can be unclear; it sometimes means that the original work has been adapted, but it is also applied to a new rendering of a figure or the creation of a new piece of art from an existing one. If a figure is revised in a minor way (color added or changed, labels altered, layout changed), it is still considered a derivative of the original or an adaptation, and permission must be obtained. If, however, a figure is cast into a new form, if the expression is new and just the basic data are retained, then permission is not needed, but the source must be cited. Some tables may be used with only a source line if the information contained in the table is factual or in the public domain. Copyright can, however, protect the compilation of the table (the unique order and sequence), and then permission would be needed. Compilation of facts in alphabetical, chronological, or numeric order is not unique; tables listing data in this manner would not need permission, only a source line.

5. News articles: News articles, as well as articles that are syndicated, under a byline, or individually copyrighted, require permission.

6. Your own previously published material: Permission from the prior publisher or copyright owner is needed if you wish to excerpt from your own previously published work.

7. Paraphrasing: The belief that paraphrasing is always legal is a myth. In reality, it may not be legal, depending on how much is paraphrased and how close it is to the original work. Changing the words is not enough if the resulting excerpt is still "substantially similar" to the original. There is no easy test to determine when you have taken only the idea and not the expression of it, but paraphrasing is particularly risky when the wording and order of presentation of material have been changed so little that a reader would recognize the similarities to the original work without difficulty.

In addition to the preceding guidelines, keep the following information in mind when deciding whether copyrighted materials require permission:

Data: Data are *not* copyrightable. What *is* copyrightable is the format in which the data are presented. If you take data from another source and present the data in an original format, permission is not needed.

Quotations within Cited Material: In reprinting articles or long portions of a book (such as material in an anthology), it is easy to overlook internal quotations from other sources. If the article contains reprinted material from another original source that requires permission according to the permissions guidelines, you must obtain separate permission for that material. This rule applies even to public domain material that includes copyrighted information. Thus, you may need several permissions to reprint one article.

Publisher Limitations: Some publishers limit the amount of material they will allow to be used in any one book. For example, W. H. Freeman limits the number of figures that can be used, and Harvard Business School Publishing restricts the number of cases. If you want to use multiple items from a single source, it is advisable to check with the source early to avoid having to make last-minute substitutions that could jeopardize your publication schedule.

Interpreting Credit Lines: Some figures and tables are not labeled "reprinted by permission" and are cited only with a source line. Words such as "from," "adapted from," and "data from" in a credit line describe how a figure or table is compiled. "From" and "adapted from" indicate that the selection is either used as it originally appeared or adapted from the original. "Data from" suggests that just facts were used from a particular source to create a new work. The citation of multiple sources may indicate that the author has created a new compilation of data; if this is the case, permission would be needed from the compiler of the data. You can see how important it is to be careful with the language of your own credit lines.

Out-of-Print Works: The fact that a work is out of print does not mean that its copyright has expired or that it is now in the public domain. Often the rights for an out-of-print work have reverted to the author of the work. Always request permission from the publisher, regardless of who holds the copyright. If necessary, the publisher will refer you to the actual copyright holder.

Fair Use

Using material without the need to obtain permission is called **fair use**. Your use of the material is considered "fair" to the original copyright holder. This is a marvelous privilege that can save time and work, but you need to use it very sparingly and only in the *few cases* where the privilege clearly applies. According to the current law, to determine whether or not the use made of a work is fair, the following factors must be considered:

1. The purpose and character of the use, including whether such use is of a commercial nature or is for nonprofit educational purposes
2. The nature of the copyrighted work
3. The amount and substantiality of the portion used in relation to the copyrighted work as a whole
4. The effect of the use upon the potential market for, or value of, the copyrighted work

As far as the length factor is concerned, Addison-Wesley usually considers quoting approximately 250 words from a book, and up to approximately 100 words from an article of a "reasonable" length, to be fair use. However, there is no recognized and agreed upon test for length or *any* of the other factors, and each case stands on its own facts.

To expand on the above factors, keep these other considerations in mind when attempting to determine if a use is fair:

- How important to the new work is the material being borrowed? If a relatively short excerpt is to become an important feature in your work, the use may not be fair.
- How important to its original source is the material being borrowed? If a relatively short excerpt is an important feature in its original source, the use may not be fair.
- Excerpting from a work that may be considered among its author's "best" may not be fair.
- Consider the "golden rule"—do unto others. Would you consider a use fair if you were the author of the original work and someone else were the borrower?

Because "fair use" is so uncertain, use it sparingly. If you need help in determining if a use is "fair," consult with the permissions editor. If you do decide that the use of certain material constitutes "fair use," you will still need to provide a full **credit line** for it in your book.

SENDING OUT PERMISSION REQUEST FORMS

Formal written permission requests should be sent as early as possible, even before you submit the manuscript to Addison-Wesley. Obtaining one permission can take up to four to six months. Use the request form shown in Figure 5.1 as a model, and type it on your own letterhead. Do not delete any part of this form.

Instructions: To be typed on author's letterhead. Words appearing in **UPPER-CASE BOLD TYPE** are to be replaced with specific project data. (**BINDING** will be replaced with "**hardbound**" or "**paperbound**"; "**#**" will be replaced with the estimated number of pages of the bound book.) **Please keep letter one page long (do not put sign-off section on a second page).**

DATE

NAME
ADDRESS

I am writing to request permission to use the material described below in my forthcoming text tentatively titled **TITLE** by **AUTHOR** (**BINDING, #** pages), to be published by Addison Wesley Longman Publishing Co. in **MONTH/YEAR**. World rights/English language are needed for all printings of this edition, including updated printings.

Description: **PLEASE INSERT A DETAILED DESCRIPTION OF THE MATERIAL YOU ARE REQUESTING PERMISSION FOR. WHENEVER POSSIBLE, ATTACH A COPY OF THE MATERIAL.**

Permission is also requested to use the same material in all current and future versions and editions of the book in all forms and media and in related supplementary and promotional materials. We also request the right to grant the material to non-profit institutions providing works for disabled students, when included in this work as a whole. Full credit will be given to the source. A release form appears below, along with space for indicating the credit line desired.

If you do not control these rights in their entirety, please let me know to whom else I must write. Thank you.

Sincerely,

NAME
POSITION

PERMISSION GRANTED:_____ _____
                              Authorized signature   Date

                        _____
                              Position
Preferred acknowledgment: _____
_____
_____

Figure 5.1 Sample permission request letter for use by authors.

If the material for which you are securing permission is also to be used in a supplement (for example, an instructor's manual or a study guide), an alternative version of your book (for example, split volumes), or in any other form or medium, electronic or otherwise, specify this in your request.

For each permission, follow these steps:

- Fill in the blanks, citing as much information as possible about the source (author, title, publisher, date, page numbers). Ask your editor or the permissions editor what territory you should request, World or North America.
- Date the letter.
- Important: Add an identifying number in the upper-right-hand corner (chapter and page number, or figure number as it will appear in *your* book).

Send the following:

- A copy of the completed *request with copies of the requested material attached* (preferably as it appears in the original source).
- If possible, a self-addressed stamped envelope or business reply envelope. This can help speed the reply.

You may find it helpful to keep a log or chart of permissions requested. *Also keep a file copy of the request sent, including attachments.*

WHAT TO DO WITH REPLIES

Scrutinize replies carefully as they arrive and take whatever action is necessary as quickly as possible.

- Sometimes the source wants to be sure that you are agreeable to its terms before granting permission. If the fee, credit line, and rights granted are acceptable, phone or write back and let the source know. You may need to sign the addressee's permission form and send it back.
- If permission from another source (for example, author, agent, or foreign publisher) is required, send a request letter to this source.
- If permission is denied, you will have to delete the selection. If another copyrighted selection is substituted, permission to use it will have to be cleared.
- If the copyright holder requests prepublication payment, or if you have any questions about the fee, consult the Addison-Wesley permissions editor.
- If you don't receive a reply in a reasonable length of time (two to three weeks), try to reach the source by phone to inquire about the status of your request.

- If a request is returned stamped "undeliverable" (for whatever reason), double-check your address. Resend the request if a new address is found. *Save the returned envelope*. In the event that the source cannot be located, we will keep this on file as evidence that a "reasonable attempt" was made to secure permission. (Note, however, that if you are unsuccessful in securing a permission, the fact that you tried does not make it permissible to use the material anyway. We will decide whether to take this risk on a case-by-case basis.)

NEGOTIATING FOR PERMISSION: CONDITIONS AND PROVISIONS

In the majority of cases, permission will be granted under certain terms and conditions. Some of these are fairly standard and accepted throughout the publishing industry; others are determined by the circumstances of the individual permission and may be negotiable. Here are the most common conditions:

Credit Line: This is not only standard and accepted, but it also helps to protect the legal rights of the copyright owner. We always use the information provided by the copyright holder, though we sometimes rearrange it for consistency.

Permission Fee: Paying a fee is an accepted condition for many kinds of permissions, and the copyright holder has the right to set any fee. However, in many cases the fee is negotiable. If you feel that the stated fee is too high, contact the source, state your point of view, and ask if they would be willing to negotiate a lower fee.

Publishers usually charge by the page for material quoted from books and journals. For individual photos, artwork, tables, and so on, a flat fee is usually charged. Poetry and songs are often charged by the line. *We will process the payment of fees upon publication of your book*, charging them as stipulated in your contract. If you absolutely *must* pay a fee in advance (some publishers ask for the fee *before* they will grant permission), please clearly mark the permission "paid" so that we don't make a duplicate payment, or send the paperwork to the permissions editor with a note asking that advance payment be made.

Complimentary Copies: Some publishers and individuals will ask to receive a copy of your book when it is published. If this condition is specified in writing, on the permission form, we will send the book upon publication.

WHAT RIGHTS DO YOU NEED?

Unless we instruct you otherwise, please request *world* rights in the *English* language for your book. If the copyright holder you initially contact does not hold full rights, you will be referred elsewhere for rights covering certain areas of the world. You'll need to send a separate request for the additional rights. Often, the copyright holder may not be willing to grant rights for "all future editions" and will limit permission to "this edition," "first edition," or "one-time use." In such cases you must obtain permission again when you prepare a new edition. We will note these limitations when you send us the completed permission forms.

WHEN ALL PERMISSIONS HAVE BEEN SECURED

The completed permission file should be sent to the permissions editor. Photocopy all forms and correspondence for your records before you send your file to us in case the originals are lost in the mail or misplaced. Each permission you send should include the following:

1. The original signed permission (may be your letter or the copyright holder's contract); include the identifying number in the upper-right-hand corner (as described above under "Sending Out Permission Request Forms").
2. If permission is granted on their contract, a copy of your request letter.
3. A copy of the material to which the permission applies.

IF YOU WERE OFFERED ASSISTANCE

If special arrangements have been made with your acquisitions editor to get help in obtaining permissions, you will need to supply the following:

1. A clear photocopy of the material from the *original source* (including page number). If you are adapting or editing the material in any way, be sure to indicate the changes on the photocopy.
2. A photocopy of the manuscript page showing how the source material is being used.
3. Photocopies of the (a) title page, (b) copyright page, and (c) acknowledgments section (if there is a separate acknowledgments section) if the mate-

rial is from a book. If the material is from a magazine, newspaper, or journal article, provide complete source information.

4. Information about the total length of the work (book, article, and so on) in
pages or number of words, so that calculations can be made to determine
if fair use is a possibility.

5. If the selection is acknowledged to another source, a copy of the acknowledgment to the original source.

Quotations and illustrations reprinted within selections (copyrighted by
someone other than the author or publisher of the selection) must be cleared separately, so you will need to provide separate information on these.

If you are preparing a new edition of an existing title, supply a list of the
selections being repeated so that permission for reuse may be requested.

PLAGIARISM

> plagiarize—to steal and pass off as one's own (the ideas or words of
> another); to present as one's own an idea or product derived from an
> existing source.
>
> *Webster's Seventh New Collegiate Dictionary*
> G. & C. Merriam Co.

Any material that is not initially created by you for your manuscript must be
accompanied by a credit line indicating its source. This holds true for material that
is adapted as well as directly excerpted. If Addison-Wesley has a permissions
review done for your manuscript, the person performing the review cannot be
expected to pick up on quoted material that you have not credited. Providing
credit lines is your responsibility.

This responsibility extends to material you may be using from your own previously published work. The quoted material is protected by the copyright of the
earlier work, and the publication rights may belong to the publisher. The material
is not original to your current manuscript and must not be represented as such.
Credit must be given and permission secured.

As discussed earlier, there are times when material is adapted or paraphrased
so extensively that it becomes a new creation. Ideas, data, and facts are not copyrightable; it is their *expression* that is copyrighted. You have to be very careful
when determining if your expression is original and not in violation of another's
copyright. Please consult the permissions editor if you want assistance in making
this determination.

PREPARING THE TEXT MANUSCRIPT

No matter how hard we all try, we cannot get away from the fact that neatness counts—for something. In this case, delivering a manuscript to us in good physical condition helps prevent problems throughout the publication process. If we cannot read your hastily penciled inserts on the side of the page, if pages that have no identifying numbers get lost, if the shipping envelope tears apart, or if you use erasable bond paper, your hard work may be wasted.

The text and illustration guidelines that we will outline in this chapter and in Chapters 7 through 9 will help you organize the contents and pedagogical devices in your text, make the reviewing process go smoothly, and ensure the acceptance of your manuscript for production. A manuscript that is hard to interpret will not review as well as one that is clear and legibly prepared, and it may be rejected by the production department.

Familiarize yourself with these instructions early on, and if someone else is typing your manuscript, be sure to share them with him or her as well. Direct your questions about these guidelines to your acquisitions or development editor, or project manager, who will put you in touch with a member of our production department.

DETERMINING MANUSCRIPT LENGTH

As you prepare your manuscript, you must consider the manuscript length and how it will translate into book pages. Book length is determined at the beginning of the project by your acquisitions editor. He or she will tell you what the total number of book pages should be, based on the topic coverage in your text and the competing texts' length. It is important that you adjust the amount of material in your manuscript so that it conforms to the total book length (including front and back matter) suggested by your editor. The exact number of book pages will depend not only on how many words you write, but also on how your book is designed and how the illustrations are treated. By working with the guidelines outlined here, you will be able to estimate book pages vis-à-vis manuscript pages, and to ensure that you are not far off the desired number of pages for the final text length, thus avoiding costly changes and delays later on.

We suggest that you do some simple calculations based on average numbers of characters per manuscript page and book page, and on approximate amounts of space for part and chapter openers, illustrations, and front and back matter. First, let's consider character counts.

CHARACTERS PER MANUSCRIPT PAGE

Rather than doing a complete character count of your manuscript, determine the average number of typed characters per manuscript page[*]:

1. On a word processor or typewriter with 10 pitch (10 characters per inch), you'll get 1320 characters per page.
2. On a word processor or typewriter with 12 pitch (12 characters per inch), you'll get 1584 characters per page.

Prepare your manuscript in a consistent format so that these character counts are valid. Do the following:

1. Use 8½ × 11-inch paper.
2. Leave 1½-inch margins all around.
3. Include 24 double-spaced lines on each manuscript page.

You will need to use the number of typed characters per page in a calculation to be described below.

CHARACTERS PER PRINTED PAGE

The number of characters on a book page varies with the trim size and the format (one column or two columns) of your text. Before you can estimate characters per printed page, you will need to speak to your acquisitions or development editor to establish these two important factors. Then use the table on the next page to estimate characters per printed book page.

---

[*]Note that most word-processing packages include a function for determining total character count.

Trim size	6¼ × 9¼	7¼ × 9¼	8 × 10	8½ × 11
One column	3200	3500	3800	4700
Two columns	———	3800	4800	5400

The number of characters per printed page will also be used in a calculation to be described below.

OTHER SPACE CONSIDERATIONS

Since few textbooks contain only straight text, other space allowances must be made. For the purpose of estimating the length of your manuscript in terms of printed book pages, use these approximations:

- Part openers (part number, part title, outline, part-opening text) = two printed pages
- Chapter openers (chapter number, chapter title, chapter outline) = one printed page (Note: if you have more material than the various elements listed here, estimate two pages.)
- Illustrations (Note: these will vary widely; use your best judgment) = ⅓ of a printed page in one-column books and ¼ of a printed page in two-column books
- Front and back matter = varies from 16 to 48 total printed pages; consult your editor for his or her best estimate

Now you will have all the numbers you need to measure your manuscript pages in terms of book pages. See the following page for an example of applying these measures in a specific case.

To estimate the length of a revised edition with tearsheet material, follow step 1 as described above. Then estimate the total number of tearsheet pages in your manuscript (assuming that both editions are the same size, one tearsheet page is the equivalent of one book page); and, as in step 2, deduct it from the total number of printed book pages desired, just as you would subtract pages for illustrations or other text elements. Proceed with the rest of the calculation as described in steps 3 and 4, but remember that the number finally yielded will reflect the pages available for newly typed copy only.

Once you arrive at the number of pages available for your final manuscript, discuss with your acquisitions editor the number of pages to assign to each chapter. Attending to this before your first draft will help you avoid having to cut copy in later drafts of the manuscript.

Keeping to your editor's suggested book length will increase your book's chances of succeeding in the market.

AN EXAMPLE

ESTIMATING PROCEDURE   EXAMPLE

Step by step, you need to do the following:

1. Find out from your acquisitions editor (a) the optimum total number of printed pages for your book; (b) the trim size; (c) the format.

(a) 632 pp
$\left\{\begin{array}{l}\text{(b) } 7\frac{3}{8} \times 9\frac{1}{4} \\ \text{(c) one column}\end{array}\right.$

2. Deduct from the number of printed pages desired the total number of pages allotted to part openers, chapter openers, front and back matter, and illustrations.

$$\begin{array}{r}(5 \text{ parts} = 10 \text{ pp}) \\ (20 \text{ chapters} = 20 \text{ pp}) \\ (\text{front and back matter} = 32 \text{ pp}) \\ (100 \text{ illus.} = \underline{33 \text{ pp}}) \\ 95 \text{ pp}\end{array}$$

$$\begin{array}{r}632 \\ -\ \underline{95} \\ 537\end{array}$$

3. Divide the projected number of characters on a printed page by the number of characters on a manuscript page. (For purposes of this example, we assume that you used a word processor getting 10 characters to the inch.)

$3500/1320 = 2.7$ (rounded off)

4. Multiply this number by the number of text pages you arrived at in step 2. This is the total number of manuscript pages your final manuscript can be.

$2.7 \times 537 = 1450$ manuscript pages (rounded off)

USING A COMPUTER

Addison-Wesley encourages all authors to use a word-processing program in the preparation of text manuscript. There are numerous advantages to using a computer, including the following:

1. As you revise your manuscript, you can generate the altered text quickly and clearly, without having to retype the material completely.

2. You can make repetitive mechanical adjustments, such as renumbering footnotes and globally correcting stylistic inconsistencies quickly and without error.

3. You can simplify the writing process by using built-in functions that help ensure the accuracy and consistency of your manuscript. These include a spelling checker, global search and replace, and automatic footnote numbering.

4. For many types of material, the **compositor** (typesetter) will be able to use your electronic files rather than rekeying.

5. For many but not all titles, we will be able to provide you with text files from the latest edition, for your use in preparing the next edition.

GUIDELINES FOR PROPER MANUSCRIPT PREPARATION

Your goal should be to submit a clean, consistently typed manuscript and, if working electronically, to provide clean files corresponding exactly to the hard copy manuscript. This will help minimize errors in your book and reduce production time. To achieve this goal, it is important that you follow these guidelines when preparing your manuscript. (Figure 6.1 shows a properly prepared manuscript page.)

1. Submit a consistently formatted manuscript with roughly the same number of characters on each manuscript page. Leave ½ inch of margin all around the text block, and type 24 text lines per page. Following these conventions will enable you and us us to estimate the length of your finished book (see the section on "Determining Manuscript Length"). Most word processors will give you approximately 1320 characters per page. If your word processor has the capability, get a precise total character count from the computer.

2. Double-space all copy, including footnotes, bibliographies, and quotations. Editors, designers, and compositors may all need to edit and add copy marks and notations to your material; the extra space will give them room. It is also important to double-space your first-draft and revised manuscripts so that the reviewers have room for comments and corrections.

3. Use the same type size and **font** for all headings and text elements (for example, lists, tables, end-of-chapter summaries and problems). Do not attempt to "design" different parts of the text, even if you can do so easily on your word processor. If you are using a typewriter, type all headings of the same level consistently, and identify the level of the head as discussed in Chapter 7. If you are working electronically and are familiar

```
                                                              2

CHAPTER ONE                      SUBMITTING A MANUSCRIPT




The material that follows shows you the proper way to submit

a manuscript.

              {A}USE THE SAME TYPE THROUGHOUT

Although you should feel free to underscore or capitalize

wherever you wish, use the same typeface, so that we can

estimate more easily the total length. At the very least,

type the same number of lines on each page and set margins

in the same place on each page. There should be 1 1/2-inch

margins all around the page.

                {A}DOUBLE-SPACE ALL COPY

Double-space all copy, even footnotes. The copyeditor needs

to edit and identify all kinds of copy, not just text; he or

she will be reading and marking footnotes,* extracts,

*Footnotes will be placed at the foot of the page on which

their reference appear. They should be double-spaced to

allow for copyediting.
```

Figure 6.1 A properly prepared manuscript page.

with your word processor's style-formatting feature, apply styles as appropriate for all headings and text elements (as above). For basal text, please name the style "text" rather than "Normal."

Consistent use of styles not only will give your document a structure that will help you organize your material but also will aid the compositor in applying the final design formatting. Unless you are preparing camera-ready copy, the styles you apply need not look like a finished book. They are included for structure only; we will have your book professionally designed and typeset.

4. If your software package has helpful features such as a spelling checker, be sure to use them. Doing so will simplify and accelerate the copyediting process.

5. Never hyphenate a word at the end of a line; use hyphens only in compound words. It is not a problem that word processors end a line at a hyphen in a compound term. However, do not use the automatic hyphenation feature of your word-processing program.

6. Use the word-wrap feature of your software (that is, automatic "carriage return" as you fill the line); use the carriage return key only at the end of a paragraph, following a title or heading, or in the construction of tables or lists. End paragraphs with one hard return. Be consistent with line spaces above or below titles and between paragraphs.

7. Use a single space at the end of a sentence. Avoid multiple spaces. Use commands built into your word-processing program for formatting paragraphs, not spaces or tabs to indicate a paragraph indent. Type **em dashes** *without* spaces before or after. If you cannot create em dashes, use two hyphens, but be consistent throughout about the spacing.

8. Use the built-in functions provided with your word-processing software for indicating emphasized (bold) text, italic type, superscripts, and subscripts.

9. Distinguish between 1s (ones) and ls (els), and between 0s (zeros) and Os (ohs).

10. Keep a log of special typing conventions used to represent unusual characters or character combinations. Use of this list will better enable Addison-Wesley editors to identify the special characters required. For mathematical or scientific presentations, many word processors have equation editors for producing mathematical symbols, Greek characters, and equations. Consult with your editor regarding the best way to handle this type of material.

11. Take advantage of the table-formatting feature that many word processors provide.

12. Incorporate all revisions in the final hard copy and disk. The manuscript you output should be clean running copy with all insertions made in the appropriate text lines. It is critical for the hard copy manuscript to match the files you supply on disk exactly.

13. Use a letter-quality printer. Make sure that the typescript is dark enough to make good photocopies. If you are unsure about the quality of your printer, ask your acquisitions editor to show a sample manuscript page to the production department as soon as you begin your first draft.

14. Consult with your editor if you plan to use your computer to create line art.

GUIDELINES FOR PROVIDING ELECTRONIC FILES

To avoid the common problems associated with disk submission, please follow these guidelines:

1. Disks and manuscript must contain the same copy. Be sure that the hard copy you supply is printed off the latest version of your disks and that it is the final version of the disks that are supplied to us.

2. Clearly label each disk with the names of the files it contains. Divide jobs into smaller, more manageable files, using "natural" breaks such as chapters. The file name should clearly indicate what is in the file; good file naming requires little guesswork about the contents of each file. A useful file name might include the first few letters of your last name, followed by the chapter number: AUTH01, AUTH02, and so on.

3. To be sure you are using an appropriate software package and disks that we can easily work with, send a sample disk and hard copy to your acquisitions or development editor before you begin keying your manuscript. Your editor can also put you in touch with our production department if you have questions. (An excellent reference for electronic manuscripts is the *Chicago Guide to Preparing Electronic Manuscripts for Authors and Publishers*, published by The University of Chicago Press.)

4. Use **virus-protection software** to avoid computer viruses that can corrupt your data and threaten our ability to produce your text. If you do not already have such software, Addison-Wesley can supply Macintosh users with freeware virus protection software at no charge. DOS and Windows users should take advantage of built-in virus-protection software that ships with DOS 5.0 or later versions.

5. Always keep backup copies of the files you send us.

6. Although in some cases we can receive files by **FTP (file transfer protocol)**, submit corresponding hard copy for editorial accuracy control reasons.

CHOOSING GOOD PAPER

Choosing good paper is as important as properly typing the manuscript. From the time the paper leaves your printer or typewriter, it goes through dozens of hands as our editors read, edit, photocopy, typemark, and transmit your manuscript within Addison Wesley Longman and to outside recipients. The message is simple: Don't use cheap paper. It just will not make it through the process.

Here are some guidelines to follow when choosing manuscript paper:

1. Use standard-size (8½ × 11-inch), 20-lb. white bond paper.
2. Do not use erasable bond or onionskin paper.
3. Make sure that every page is the same size. Smaller paper will get lost, and larger paper will tear apart.

Numbering Your Pages

With hundreds of manuscript pages piling up on your desk, it is essential to develop a foolproof numbering system before you begin writing. We recommend the following:

1. Within each chapter, number your draft manuscript consecutively with double numbers (for example, 10-1, 10-2). Number the final manuscript consecutively in the upper-right-hand corner of each page.
2. Number your front matter manuscript and illustration manuscript separately. (We will discuss these elements further in Chapters 8 and 9.) However, number the back matter consecutively with the final text manuscript.
3. In order to identify all subsequent drafts easily, add the date to the first page of each chapter.

If you need to add pages at the last minute, do the following:

1. Designate the inserted pages with the number of the preceding page plus a, b, c, and so on; for example, 10a, 10b, 10c. At the top of the preceding numbered page, note the lettered pages that follow; for example, on top of page 10, write "pages 10a and 10b follow." Try to keep inserted pages to a minimum.
2. If you delete a page after the manuscript is numbered, assign two numbers to the preceding page, or note the deletion. For example, if you delete page 11, number page 10 "10 and 11"; or write on page 10, "page 12 follows."

Corrections and Insertions

After your manuscript has been keyed, you will most likely need to make corrections. If you are using a word-processing program, simply incorporate all revisions into the disk, and provide hard copy that includes all of your corrections. If your manuscript was prepared on a typewriter, or if you want to make minor corrections to word-processed copy, follow these guidelines (Figure 6.2 on page 44 shows you the proper way to correct manuscript copy):

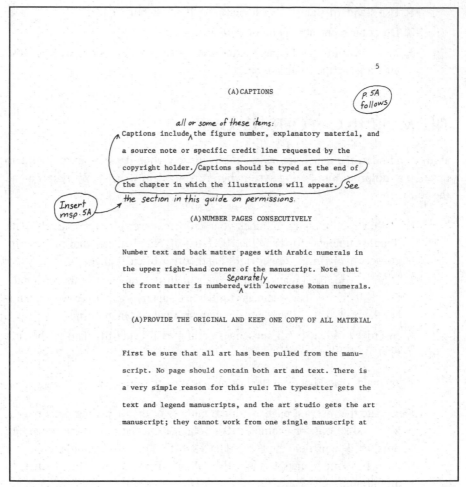

Figure 6.2 A manuscript page prepared on a typewriter, with corrections properly marked.

1. Type brief changes or corrections above the line in which they should appear. Handwritten changes are permitted if they are very brief and printed clearly in ink. These should be kept to a minimum.

2. Retype all heavily revised pages.

3. Type lengthy insertions on separate pages and clearly identify where they are to be placed in the text. For example, to change a heavily revised paragraph that appears on page 20, type the revised copy on a new sheet, number it 20a, and write on top, "insert for msp. 20" (*msp.* stands for "manuscript page"). On the original manuscript page, msp. 20, write "insert page 20a" at the precise location of the change.

4. If several insertions are to be added to one manuscript page, type them all on one insert page. Identify each insert in some way so that placement on the preceding manuscript page is apparent (for example, "insert A,"

"insert B," and so on.) Key your insertions for different manuscript pages on separate insert pages.

5. Regardless of their length, do not make changes or corrections in the margins, on tags attached to the manuscript pages, or on the backs of pages

MANUSCRIPTS CONTAINING PREVIOUSLY PUBLISHED MATERIAL

Some books, such as collections of case studies, contain previously published, or "reprint," material. Reprint material may also appear in discrete sections of a textbook; for example, in a special feature occurring once in a chapter. Prepare all reprint material as follows:

1. Do not retype reprinted copy; submit tearsheets or legible photocopies of tearsheets. (**Tearsheets** are pages torn from a bound book.)
2. Affix tearsheets on standard-size (8½ × 11) paper with "magic" type tape (the kind of tape you can write on), on one side of the page only.
3. If the type on the tearsheets has been set in two or more columns, cut the columns apart and paste each column on a separate page.
4. If there are legends and illustrations in the tearsheets that you would like to use, cut them out and prepare them separately (see Chapters 7 and 9). If you do not want to use them, simply cross them out.
5. If both sides of the book page are needed, submit either two tearsheets of the same page or one tearsheet and one photocopy.
6. When submitting photocopies of book pages, make sure that they are perfectly clear and standard 8½ × 11-inch size. Nonstandard-size photocopies must be pasted up in the same way as tearsheets, on 8½ × 11-inch paper.
7. When pasting up tearsheets or photocopies of tearsheets, do not delete the original printed page number, even though you will be numbering the page with your own manuscript page number. (We may need to refer to the original page number—for example, if permission is needed to use the material.)

All new copy to be inserted within the body of reprint material must be set off by brackets. Omissions must be clearly indicated in the following way:

1. Use three centered dots between paragraphs to indicate the omission of one or more entire paragraphs.
2. Begin a paragraph with ellipses (three spaced dots) if the beginning of the original paragraph has been omitted, regardless of how much preceding material may have been omitted.

3. End a paragraph with ellipses if the end of the original paragraph has been omitted.

4. Use ellipses to indicate omissions of any length within a paragraph or line.

When using reprint material, be sure to obtain permission if necessary, according to the guidelines given in Chapter 5.

Turning Over the Final Manuscript to Production

Your final manuscript is not complete without the cleared permissions, the front matter and back matter, the art program (line art and photographs), and the captions (see Chapters 5 and 8–9). We can turn final manuscript over to production in "batches," but each batch must represent at least one-quarter of the total manuscript. The batches must be submitted to production in order, with all text elements—text, boxes, references, illustrations, and so on—included. The first batch should be accompanied by the table of contents for the whole book, and the last batch must include the front matter and end matter.

Shipping the Final Manuscript

Make one copy of all the material you are submitting, and keep it for yourself. Send us the *original* version. Be sure that all copies reflect final changes in your manuscript. Do not bind, clip, or staple the manuscript. Instead, put a rubber band around each part of the manuscript, separating the text manuscript, art manuscript, and so on, into separate piles.

Ship the manuscript in a sturdy cardboard box; do not send it in manila envelopes. Include a second Addison-Wesley mailing label in each box you send us so that if the outer wrapping or label is destroyed, the mailing service can still get the material to us.

Take special care in shipping photos or camera-ready art. Never fold or bend them. Protect them with strong cardboard. If an illustration cannot be packed flat, it should be rolled and inserted in a cardboard tube. These precautions are necessary, because any tears, folds, scratches, or marks on final illustration copy will show up when it is reproduced for printing in the book (see Chapter 9).

Ship all manuscript and illustrations in the fastest and safest way possible. Generally, we suggest using an overnight or two-day delivery service such as UPS or Federal Express. Always use a traceable service.

PREPARING THE TEXT ELEMENTS

The text elements we will discuss in this chapter have a single, critical purpose: to make it easy for students to understand and learn the material. Elements such as parts and chapters, internal text headings, lists, and tables help present the subject logically and break up long stretches of text. Your job is to use this pedagogy in a consistent way throughout the text and to type it consistently in the manuscript. A clear presentation will help us design each page properly and will reduce the possibility of any errors.

Unless you are preparing camera-ready copy, when using a word-processing program do not format your material to make it look more attractive or more like it will in final book form (such as the use of different type fonts, rules or icons, and excessive spacing and tabs). Any formatting you impose will need to be stripped out so our own design can be implemented. It is best, therefore, that you keyboard your manuscript using only boldface and underlining as necessary. In the case of mathematics manuscripts, use italics for variables.

BEGINNING A NEW PART OR CHAPTER

Chapters are your basic elements of organization. They divide the material into distinct sections that correspond with the way instructors teach the course. Parts group several related chapters together to form a unit of material. Follow these guidelines when working with these elements:

1. Start each new part title on a new page with the part number and title near the top of the page. If your have written special text to introduce the part, start it on the same page as the part number and title.
2. Begin each new chapter on a new page, placing the chapter number and title near the top of the page.

3. Get your editor's approval before including special pedagogical devices in part and chapter openers, such as outlines and learning objectives. Organize and key them consistently throughout your manuscript.

4. Organize publications such as workbooks in units and sections rather than parts and chapters. Arrange units and sections as described for parts and chapters.

TEXT HEADINGS

Headings break up the text and help students understand the material. As a rule, they should be short phrases or single words, not sentences. Generally, three levels of headings are sufficient for a well-organized textbook. Headings should generally not occur together without text between them, and good structure dictates that there should be more than one subhead to a section to legitimize dividing it up. Be consistent in the frequency and use of headings from one chapter to another. For example, if you begin one chapter with a heading, do so in all other chapters. It will be most helpful to the copyeditor, designer, and compositor if you type all headings of the same value in a consistent way.

{A} A-HEADS

First-level heads (or A-heads) are the main chapter heads; type them on a line alone, centered on the page, in uppercase and lowercase letters. Leave one line of space above and below. In addition, label the heading with its value by typing {A} preceding the heading.

Traditionally, first-level headings are numbered in math and some science texts. Double numbers, consecutive within chapters, are used. For example, 1.6 would designate the sixth A-head in Chapter 1.

{B} B-HEADS

Second-level heads (or B-heads) are subdivisions of the first-level head; position them on a line alone, flush left on the page, and in uppercase and lowercase letters. Leave one line of space above and below. Label each B-head with a {B} preceding the heading. Because B-heads are subdivisions of A-heads, they should only be used when an A-head has previously been introduced.

{C} C-Heads. The third-level head is positioned as a "run-in" heading. Type it on a paragraph indent, in uppercase and lowercase letters, and run into the text that follows. Leave one line of space above. Label each C-head with a {C} preceding the heading.

In some textbooks, particularly in technical disciplines, additional head levels or types of headings may be required. You should discuss the styling of such headings with your acquisitions or development editor. Type all headings of equal value in the same way.

TABLES

Tables present certain material, especially numerical data, more clearly and concisely than text (see Figure 7.1). However, if tables are not well constructed, they can be more confusing than helpful. *The Chicago Manual* has an excellent section on table preparation, with more detail and examples than can possibly be presented here. Our guidelines pertain only to the appearance and typing of the table elements. The following list contains the basic elements found in tables:

1. *Numbers and titles.* Most tables should be double-numbered by chapter (for example, Table 1.1, Table 2.3) and given a brief title that precisely describes the content. If a table consists of only a few entries and two or three columns, it may not need to be titled and numbered.
2. *Text references and table placement.* Refer to all numbered tables in the text. In the printed book, tables always follow their text reference as closely as possible. Simple unnumbered tabular material needs no formal in-text reference, although the relevance of the table should be obvious from the text discussion.

Table 9.1 Economic Dimensions of the Bond Market, 1980 to 1990

Type of Issuer[a]	Year-End Amounts Outstanding (in billions)		
	1980	1985	1990
U.S. Treasury	$159.8	$ 427.0	$1,023.6
U.S. agencies	17.6	276.1	447.3
States and municipalities	144.4	322.3	734.9
Corporations	181.0	421.7	752.3
Total	$502.8	$1,447.1	$2,958.1

[a]Excludes institutional issues as such data are not available.

Sources: <u>Federal Reserve Bulletin</u>, <u>U.S. Treasury Bulletin</u>, and <u>Survey of Current Business</u>.

Figure 7.1 A well-prepared table.

3. *Column heads*. Keep column heads short. Single-word column heads are best, and abbreviations should be used whenever possible. If notations such as "percentage" or "in dollars" apply to all the material in a table, add them following the table title or as a footnote rather than repeating them in the column heads. Use rules to separate levels of column heads, and style column heads consistently in all tables.

4. *Body of the table*. All tables should be double-spaced to facilitate copy-editing and updating of files. Words in table columns should line up at the left, with subentries and turning lines indented a few spaces consistently. Numbers in columns should line up on the right, on the decimal point, or on the dash in a range of numbers.

5. *Table rules*. Rules—thin separating lines—should appear below the number and title, below the column heads, and below the body of the table. They should span the width of the table body. Avoid additional horizontal rules (except for short rules for levels of column headings) and vertical rules in the body of the table.

6. *Notes*. If there is any information that applies to the entire table (for example, how data were gathered), write it in a general note, preceded by the word *Note(s)*. Position it right below the body of the table (after the rule).

7. *Footnotes*. Place **footnotes** below the general note or right below the body of the table (after the rule), and number them with superscript lowercase italic letters (*a, b, c*), consecutively within the table. (Superscript notations are placed above the normal line of type.) **Footnote references** (also superscript lowercase italic letters) in the tables read horizontally across the columns, not vertically within a column. Be sure every footnote has an in-table footnote reference.

8. *Source notes and credit lines*. For tables taken from previously published material, complete data for each source must appear below the table, after any notes or footnotes. Op. cit. or ibid. cannot be used even if a previous table is from the same source. Precede the **source note** with the word *Source(s)*.

Quotations and Extracts

Short **quotations** (less than three typeset lines) should run-in with the text, surrounded by quotation marks. **Extracts** refer to previously published text quotations that are at least five or more lines when typeset and therefore need to be set off (displayed) from the regular text. Quotations of even one line of poetry or a song should also be set up as extracts. (See Chapter 5 for information on obtaining permission for the use of extracted material.) Follow these rules when you include a displayed extract in your manuscript:

1. Begin the extract on a new line, indented from the left.
2. Align the rest of the extract on this indent as a block of type. For extracts of more than one paragraph, indent subsequent paragraphs.
3. Quotation marks are not required at the beginning or end of the displayed extract, but if any words within the extract appeared in quotation marks in the original source, use double quotation marks for those same words (even if single marks were used originally).
4. Double-space all extracts.

The following rules apply to both quotations and extracts:

1. If words or lines that appeared in the original source are being omitted, indicate this with three spaced ellipsis dots in the middle of a sentence and four dots between sentences. If the sentence preceding the omitted sentence(s) ends with a question mark or an exclamation point in the original, keep the mark in the extract and follow it with three ellipsis dots.
2. Some changes from the source material are allowed. They must be enclosed in square brackets in the quotation/extract or explained in the source note for the quotation/extract or in the preceding text.
3. All quotations and extracts require full source information in the form of a footnote (footnotes will be discussed later in the chapter).

The Chicago Manual has a comprehensive section on quotations and extracts; if you have many in your text, you may want to consult it. One final note: It is essential that the quoted material you use in your book be completely accurate. Double-check all quoted material against the original source prior to submitting your manuscript for production. You are the only one who can ensure the accuracy of quoted material.

LISTS

Lists may be written as (1) regular text, (2) numbered items set off from regular text, (3) bulleted items set off from regular text, (4) unnumbered items set off from regular text, (5) items in outline format set off from regular text, or (6) numbered text paragraphs. The preceding sentence is an example of a list written as regular text. If you want to set off a list from its preceding text, remember the following:

1. Indent listed sentences or words from the left.
2. Leave extra space above and below the entire list.
3. Double-space lists as you would regular text.
4. Type lists consistently throughout the manuscript.
5. Style items within lists consistently; within a particular list, each item should be an entire sentence, or each item should be only a phrase.
6. Punctuate the ends of sentence items with the appropriate punctuation. Lists of single words or phrases should not be punctuated. Do not link displayed (set off) items with commas, semicolons, and/or a conjunction.

These instructions are an example of the way a **numbered list** should be presented. Use numbered lists particularly for lists with a set number of items or a set sequence. Unnumbered or bulleted lists can be treated the same way, without the numbers. Outline lists should follow proper form for such lists (see *The Chicago Manual*). **Numbered paragraphs** are used for lengthier discussions and presentations (that is, not simply a quick list of items) that need to be numbered but are too cumbersome to set off from the main text in the same way as a numbered list; numbered paragraphs should not be indented or set apart with space above and below.

FOOTNOTES, NOTES, AND REFERENCES

SUBSTANTIVE FOOTNOTES

Substantive footnotes are editorial comments that are necessary to the understanding of the text. They should be used sparingly; if you find you are using them frequently, you may need to expand the text explanations instead.

When substantive footnotes are necessary, type them double-spaced at the bottom of the manuscript page on which their references appear. The footnotes on a particular page should be referenced with a series of superscript symbols: an asterisk (*) for the first one, a dagger (†) for the second, a double dagger (‡) for the third, and a section mark (§) for the fourth. If you need more than these you are probably relying too heavily on footnotes and should incorporate some of the material in the text discussion. Begin each new sequence of footnotes on a page with an asterisk.

If you begin a footnote at the bottom of a page and run out of space, continue it on a separate manuscript page, by itself, with no other text. Number the page along with the rest of the manuscript.

For both substantive footnotes and bibliographical notes (see the following section) avoid footnoting part or chapter titles or any other displayed headings.

BIBLIOGRAPHICAL NOTES

Bibliographical notes cite sources for statements or quotations in the text. Rather than placing them at the bottom of pages (which, if there are many, may interrupt the flow of reading and create page makeup problems), group them together at the end of the chapter. The notes should be numbered consecutively with single arabic numerals beginning with "1" in each chapter. At the text reference, note numbers should be in superscript position. Do not enclose them in parentheses or punctuate them. The text of the bibliographical notes should be grouped in numerical order at the end of the chapter, double-spaced, starting on a new page. The bibliographical notes should follow end-of-chapter material such as the summary, key words listing, and review questions, but should precede any listing of general references. Begin each note on a new line; the numbers should not be superscript, but set on the baseline with a period following. The note pages should be numbered along with the rest of the manuscript.

Be sure to choose one style for notes, use it consistently, and always give complete information. According to *The Chicago Manual*, a full bibliographical note should include the following items, listed in the order in which they are usually given:

BOOK

Author's full name

Complete title of the book

Editor, compiler, or translator, if any

Series, if any, and volume or number in the series

Edition, if not the original

Number of volumes

Facts of publication—city where published, publisher, date of publication

Volume number, if any

Page number(s) of the particular citation

ARTICLE IN A PERIODICAL

Author's full name

Title of the article

Name of the periodical

Volume (and number) of the periodical

Date of the volume or of the issue

Page number(s) of the particular citation

UNPUBLISHED MATERIAL
Title of document, if any, and date
Folio number or other identifying number
Name of collection
Depository, and city where it is located

AUTHOR-DATE REFERENCES

In some disciplines, an **author-date reference** system for citing sources is pre-ferred. Authors' names and publication dates are cited within the text, enclosed in parentheses [for example, "(Smith 1996)"]. The complete bibliographical informa-tion is grouped alphabetically by author in a reference section at the end of each chapter or at the end of the book, depending on the conventions of your discipline.

As noted previously, certain disciplines have their own bibliographical style, such as APA or MLA. It is most important to style the references consistently and give complete information. Although it may seem like a lot of work in the beginning, you will have to consult the source only once; otherwise you will have to go back to the source for missing information when you review the copyedited manuscript.

CAPTIONS

Although captions (formerly known as legends) appear with illustrations in the printed book, they must be separated from the illustrations, for production pur-poses, at the manuscript stage. Follow these guidelines:

1. Captions for illustrations should be double-numbered, corresponding to the figure numbers, and both must be consistent with the references with-in the text. Captions for unnumbered illustrations (those not referenced in the text) should be numbered for identification purposes with the chapter number and a capital letter (for example, 12A, 12B, and so on); these numbers will not appear in the final book. If both numbered and unnum-bered illustrations appear in your manuscript, you need to provide two caption manuscripts, one with captions for numbered illustrations, and one with captions for unnumbered illustrations. Consult your editor if you are unsure whether to prepare more than one caption manuscript.

2. If an illustration has (a) and (b) parts, be sure the caption has both descrip-tions.

3. The captions for each chapter should be placed at the end of the text manu-script in the chapter in which the illustration will appear, after any other

end-of-chapter text elements such as the bzibliography. Captions should be double-spaced and numbered in sequence with the text manuscript.

4. Illustrations without captions should be listed as well, in sequential order, followed by the words "no caption."

5. Credit lines or source notes (for illustrations taken from previously published material) should be included at the end of each caption (see Chapter 5). Be sure to check permissions letters for specific wording of credit lines.

OTHER PEDAGOGICAL AIDS

Many special text elements (boxes, cases, essays) are not part of the running text and may be placed near an appropriate text discussion, not in any precise spot. It is best to double-number them as you do tables and illustrations. (Follow the instructions for unnumbered illustrations if you do not wish to number your special text elements.) Like an illustration call-out, a call-out in parentheses should be added on a separate line below the paragraph in which the element is referenced, or, if the element is not referenced directly in the text, add the call-out between two text paragraphs approximately where you would like the element to appear.

TECHNICAL MATERIAL

It is expected that most authors of technical manuscripts will be using the International System of Units (SI) for measurements. Standards on abbreviations and usage have been published in various documents and by academic associations. Please refer to them as you prepare your manuscript, and let us know which authority you use, so that we can refer to the same one during the copyediting process. For specific style points governing the use of numerals, punctuation of technical material, display of equations, where to break equations, and use of fractions, see the latest edition of *The Chicago Manual* and the *Addison-Wesley Mathematics Typesetting Style Guide*. A few major points are discussed here.

EQUATIONS

Equations that are long, complex, and, of course, important should be displayed. Type them centered on the page, with one line of space above the first line of the equation, one line of space below the last line of the equation, and one line of space between equation lines. If there are two short equations that should appear together, type them on the same line, with enough space between them so it is clear that they are separate. Regardless of whether you are numbering all or only the most important equations, number the equations consecutively within sections [as (1), (2), (3)], and so on. You could also use the same double-numbering system assigned to tables, figures, and other numbered pedagogy in your manuscript. Equation numbers should be enclosed in parentheses and positioned at the right margin. Within equations (and technical copy in running text), leave space around operation and relation signs; trigonometric and logarithmic functions; arrows; integral, summation, and product signs; before a delta and a unit of measure; and after a comma. Coefficients and terms to be multiplied should be typed closed up, without space. Here are some examples:

$$x + y + z = 0$$

$$(x, y)$$

$$4x + 3y = 22$$

$$2H_2O$$

$$x \int y \, dt \qquad \sin x \qquad \log x \qquad 2 \tan x$$

Exceptions:

   $+3$ (The sign designates a positive

   -2 or a negative quantity.)

For more examples of spacing, see the *Addison-Wesley Mathematics Typesetting Style Guide*.

FRACTIONS

When fractions are set within text lines, they will be set as **solidus**; for example, $(a + b)/(c + d)$. In this case, be sure to insert parentheses wherever necessary to avoid any ambiguity. In displayed material, all but the simplest fractions will be set built up:

$$\frac{a+b}{c+d}$$

SUBSCRIPTS AND SUPERSCRIPTS

Type **subscripts** (characters placed below the normal line of type) and **superscripts** (characters placed above the normal line of type) in the appropriate position; but if they are in the least bit unclear, mark them as well. This also applies to degree signs, primes, and valences in chemistry. Here are several examples, with some of them marked:

$$a_x{}^y \qquad a_x{}' \qquad a^{1/2} \qquad a_{\widehat{K,q+1}} \qquad H_2O \qquad a_{h_{\widehat{2}}}$$

BOLDFACE LETTERS, GREEK LETTERS, SCRIPT LETTERS, SMALL CAPS

For special uses of letters for symbols, clarity is most important. If you cannot type boldface letters, Greek letters, or script letters on your word processor, write in the

letter you want and identify the Greek or script in the margin, next to its first occurrence on the page. For boldface, draw a wavy line below the typed letter (A̰); for
small caps, draw two underscores below a typed capital letter (A̲). Mark for italic
letters using the underscore if you cannot type italic letters.

OTHER SPECIAL SYMBOLS

Any other special mathematical or chemical symbols should be identified in the
margin next to their first occurrence on the page. You may even have to differentiate
between a 0 (zero) and a capital O (oh) if your typescript does not clearly do this.
Other symbols and letters that are frequently confused if not identified include:

> one and "el"
> "ex" and Greek chi
> "en" and lowercase Greek eta
> "vee" and lowercase Greek nu
> "double-u" and lowercase Greek omega
> "element of" and lowercase Greek epsilon
> summation sign and capital Greek sigma
> product sign and capital Greek pi
> proportional sign and lowercase Greek alpha

Be sure to clarify with a written note in the margin all of these, and others,
when they first appear.

Eight

PREPARING THE FRONT MATTER AND BACK MATTER

FRONT MATTER

Front matter is all material preceding the first page of Part 1 or Chapter 1. It should be submitted along with the text and prepared in the same manner as the text, with the exception of page numbering. Begin front matter with roman numeral "i"; begin the first page of text with arabic numeral "1."

Front matter can consist of many different elements. You must include at least a title page, table of contents, and preface (in that order). The copyright page will be prepared by Addison Wesley Longman. It will appear after the title page.

HALF TITLE PAGE

Frequently, a **half title page** is included. This page comprises *only* the book's full title (but not the subtitle), and occupies page i. If you are supplying camera-ready copy, page ii would be blank and the full title page would fall on page iii.

TITLE PAGE

The **title page** should include the complete main title of the book, the subtitle (if any), edition (if other than first), your name exactly as you wish it to appear in print, and the official name of your affiliation. Be sure that the wording and punctuation of your affiliation are accurate (for example, University of California, Berkeley). If there are several authors, be sure to provide the affiliations for each. Although the publisher's name and logo also appear on the title page, you do not need to provide this copy; we provide it.

TABLE OF CONTENTS

The **table of contents** (or contents) must include at least all part titles (if any), chapter titles, and first-level text heads. Check with your acquisitions editor to see if second- and, possibly, third-level heads should be included as well. Even if second- and third-level heads will not ultimately be included in the contents, it is very helpful for us to have a complete table of contents to which we can refer throughout the production process. (Including manuscript page numbers next to heads is also useful.) Before you submit the final manuscript, double-check the contents against the manuscript to be sure that there is agreement. (See Figure 8.1 on page 60 for an example of a table of contents page.)

In addition to the detailed table of contents, some disciplines require a **brief table of contents**, or brief contents, listing the front matter elements, part and chapter titles, and back matter elements. This is especially important as a quick reference if the detailed contents will include several levels of heading. Please consult your acquisitions editor or project manager if you are uncertain whether to include both types of contents.

PREFACE

The **preface** is a selling and marketing tool and thus should be written with care. Because it should be a concise and positive statement about the book as you wrote it, it must be written last. It will be read by faculty looking for a summary of what the book is about, why you wrote it, and what is special about your text. It will also be read by sales representatives needing a quick rebriefing before making sales calls or presentations.

The preface should start with the rationale or approach of your book. Be sure to discuss what makes your text unique and better than other books. What are its special features, and how will they benefit students and faculty? Also cover the supplements, if any, and describe what is special about them (your acquisitions editor can help you with this). If you are writing a revision, the preface must explain what is new to this edition and why you made the changes. Be aware of your audience. If you want to write something to students, do so in a separate preface entitled "To the Student."

Acknowledgments, or words of thanks to reviewers and others who helped you develop and prepare your manuscript, will be placed at the end of the preface. (Your acquisitions editor or development editor will supply names and affiliations of all reviewers.) Note that these acknowledgments differ from acknowledgments you may need to give to publishers and authors who granted you permission to reprint previously published material.

Discuss the preface with your acquisitions or development editor and be prepared for some substantial commentary. Editors look for clean, upbeat prefaces that capture the essence of the book's features, strengths, and pedagogical

CONTENTS

Preface

PART ONE   Preparation of Manuscript

CHAPTER 1   Submitting a Manuscript

              Type Consistently

                  Double-Space All Copy

                  Type Headings Consistently

                  Number all Figures

                  Prepare a Separate Legend Manuscript

              Number Pages Consecutively

              Provide Us with an Original Copy

              Obtain Permissions

CHAPTER 2   Submitting an Art Manuscript

              Categorize the Types of Illustrations

                  Line Art

                  Photographs

                  Camera Copy

                  Maps

                  Cartoons

              Provide a Visual for Each Numbered and

              Unnumbered Illustration

Figure 8.1 A table of contents page listing parts, chapters, and two levels of headings.

effectiveness. Do not advertise what the book does not have, and avoid an apologetic or defensive tone.

ADDITIONAL ELEMENTS

You may also choose to include the following elements in your front matter.

    Credits and Acknowledgments This refers to acknowledgments to publishers and authors who granted you permission to reprint their material. If the acknowledgments (or credit lines) do not appear on the text page on which the material falls, they can be grouped together on the copyright page or directly following the copyright page. (If there are many acknowledgments, they may be included in the back matter.) It is common to begin the section with a statement such as, "Grateful acknowledgment is made for use of the following material."

Dedication Include a dedication if you desire. A **dedication** is a personal message of thanks, usually given to a special person or persons who helped you on the project. Many of our authors dedicate their texts to close family members or colleagues who proved essential in writing the text. The dedication page usually follows the copyright page. (The dedication may be placed on the copyright page, if we find that we need to conserve space when we calculate the total page count.)

Back Matter

Back matter is all material following the last page of the main portion of the text. Except for the index, which is prepared later in the production process, back matter manuscript should be submitted along with the main text manuscript. It is important that the back matter travel with the text because the copyeditor must check text references and glossary entries for consistency with the back matter. Back matter manuscript should be consecutively numbered and include a prefix, such as BM-1, BM-2, and so on.

Back matter goes through the same stages of production as regular text. Therefore, guidelines you follow in preparing the main portion of the text (including double-spaced typing) apply to the back matter as well.

Back matter can include the following elements: appendixes, answers or solutions to in-text questions and exercises, author-date references, a glossary, a bibliography, and indexes. Note that except for indexes, some or all of these elements may be placed at the end of chapters instead of at the end of the book. Regardless of where you place them, you should prepare the back matter manuscript in the same fashion as regular text.

APPENDIXES

Appendixes contain material related to the text but set apart from it. If there is more than one appendix, each one should be numbered (Appendix 1, Appendix 2, and so on) or lettered (Appendix A, Appendix B, and so on). They should also be given titles.

ANSWERS TO IN-TEXT QUESTIONS AND PROBLEMS

In some disciplines, answers to some or all of the questions and problems within the text are provided in the back matter. These should be prepared consistently and proofread carefully; if the solutions involve illustrations or equations, make sure that the presentation is consistent with the text presentation. As noted elsewhere in this *Guide*, it is easiest to prepare the solutions at the same time you are writing the problems, to avoid having to do all of them at once.

AUTHOR-DATE REFERENCES

When an author-date reference section is not included at the end of each chapter, it may be placed at the end of the book. There the references can be arranged by chapter or combined into one comprehensive list. Within each section, always list references alphabetically by author. (See the examples that follow for bibliographical entries.)

GLOSSARY

In general, key terms that are emphasized in the text (with boldface or italic type) or grouped at the end of the chapter are defined in the **glossary**. Terms to be defined in the glossary should be arranged in alphabetical order in your glossary manuscript. Each item should begin on a new line and be followed by its definition. Like the solutions, the glossary is ideally prepared as you are writing the text, both to avoid an enormous task at the end and to ensure consistency between the glossary definitions and the text definitions. Please check with your acquisitions or development editor if you plan both an end-of-chapter glossary and an end-of-text glossary.

BIBLIOGRAPHY

Bibliographies, which list all the publications you used to write the text, as well as additional readings, can take various forms. The most common type of bibliography is arranged alphabetically by authors' last names. [Unlike bibliographical notes (see Chapter 7), entries in a bibliography need no numbering.] According to *The Chicago Manual*, a full bibliographical reference should include the following items, in this order:

BOOK

Name of the author(s), the editor(s), or the institution responsible for the writing of the book

Full title of the book, including the subtitle, if any

Title of series, if any, and volume or number in the series

Volume number or total number of volumes of a multivolume work

Edition, if not the original

City of publication

Publisher's name

Date of publication

ARTICLE IN A PERIODICAL

Name of the author(s)

Title of the article

Name of the periodical

Volume number (sometimes issue number)

Date

Pages occupied by the article

Examples of bibliographical entries follow:

Gitman, Lawrence J. *Principles of Managerial Finance*, Brief Edition. Reading, Mass.: Addison-Wesley, 1998.

Angel, Allen R. and Stuart R. Porter. *A Survey of Mathematics with Applications,* Fifth Edition. Reading, Mass.: Addison-Wesley, 1997.

A bibliography can be set up in other ways. It may a **selected bibliography**—broken into sections by subject. It may take the form of an **annotated bibliography**, with the annotations typed directly below the bibliographic entry. Or it may be a discursive **bibliographical essay**, in which sources are discussed in a narrative form.

INDEXES

An **index** gives your readers access to the material in your book by providing page references for all important ideas, people, events, and so on. Many books have a subject index. A **subject index** includes entries for both proper names and subjects. Some books also feature an **author index**, which contains the name of all authors cited in the book.

The most essential question to consider when creating index entries is, What terms would *readers* have in mind? Including terms that provide multiple points of access for a range of readers is the foundation for a successful index.

Indexing: The Basic Steps. The best way to index is to break the process down into four steps.

Step 1: Read and Mark Proof Pages. Underline or highlight anything you think might serve as a main entry. Specify subentries by underlining, circling, or writing in the margin. Specify a subentry for almost every main entry. It is much easier to delete unnecessary subentries than to search back through the text, trying to categorize a long series of page references. Write cross-references in the margins as they occur to you.

This step corresponds to writing an outline for a book. As you underline, the structure of the index—the main entries—subentries, cross-references, and level of detail or generality—will emerge. Read through the pages as rapidly as possible, focusing on the structural relationships of the information. Leave difficult decisions for the keying and reviewing stages.

Step 2: Key Entries into the Computer. This step is like writing a first draft. Decide which terms will be main entries and which will be cross-references. Decide which subentries should be main entries as well. Enter all cross-references that occur to you.

There is special indexing software that alphabetizes, punctuates, combines entries, and facilitates editing. The American Society of Indexers publishes an annual review of indexing software. If you do not have indexing software, do not use the indexing feature that comes with your word processor. Enter terms into a blank file. Type in each new term in its correct alphabetical place. If you do not have a computer, see *The Chicago Manual* for instructions on how to use index cards.

Step 3: Review the Index. Print out the index in alphabetical order and edit it. This step is like revising text. Refine your categories. Clarify overlapping and related terms. Break down long series of page numbers by adding subentries. Delete and combine subentries. Delete references to identical material. Add cross-references.

Step 4: Final Editing. Read over the index for style and clarity. Check alphabetization and consistency of cross-references, and then proofread the index.

What to Index. In addition to indexing the body of the text, index any notes that contain new information, but do not index notes that merely cite sources. Index important tables and illustrations that appear on a different page from the text describing them. Do not make special note of the fact that information appears in a table, illustration, or example. Index important material from the appendixes. Do not index the bibliography or glossary. Index the terms in the glossary but send the reader to the text page where they are defined.

Selecting Main Entries. Again, the cardinal rule of indexing is, "Put yourself in the place of your readers." When choosing main entries, ask yourself what word or phrase readers would have in mind. Provide different points of access for different readers by using more than one main entry for important concepts. Be thorough—index every important piece of information—but at the same time be selective. Don't index discussions that are merely examples or passing references. Don't send readers to identical material repeated on different pages. Be concise. Your task as an indexer is to refer to a page, not to inform about a topic. Try to restrict the main entry to one or two words. The title or subject of a book is usually too general to use as a main entry.

Selecting Subentries. When the main entry covers many pages, use subentries to direct the reader to specific aspects of the topic. Any entry with more than five page references needs subentries. Do not have a long list of subentries that repeat the same page numbers. Instead, convert some of those subentries into main entries in order to provide more points of access to the audience.

EXAMPLE	BETTER
Habitats, 20	Desert, 20
desert, 20	Habitats, 20
rainforest, 20	Rainforest, 20
tundra, 20	Tundra, 20

Choose the right level of generality. Don't include every detail as a subentry. Find a term general enough to cover several aspects of the topic. Consolidate subentries by combining specific references under a more general heading.

EXAMPLE	BETTER
Dogs	Dogs, 11–15
bathing, 15	grooming,
breeds, 11–13	14–15
clipping and combing, 14	selecting,
commands, 22, 24	11–13
pedigrees, 13	training,
sending to obedience	22–24
school, 22	
tricks, 24	

Do not use sub-subentries.

Selecting Cross-references. Cross-references refer the reader to other entries. They may be synonyms used in the text, technical synonyms for common words, common synonyms for technical words, or shortened or inverted entries. Cross-references may also refer to related material or to more specific or more general entries. They do not have to mean the same thing as the main entry.

There are two types, *See* and *See also*. *See* cross-references contain no page numbers; they simply point to an alternative entry. *See also* cross-references contain at least one page number, and the entry they lead to provides additional page numbers. Do not send the reader to entries that contain new terms but no new page numbers. When an entry is short, don't cross-reference. Instead, repeat the page numbers.

Using Page References. Page references placed directly after the main entry often signal the most important information. A large span of page numbers can indicate a section or chapter devoted to the topic. You are not required to include any page numbers after the main entry.

Style. Use line-for-line style. The main entry begins on the first line. Each subentry begins on a new, indented line. *See* cross-references follow the main entry, separated by a period. *See also* cross-references follow the subentries on a new indented line, separated by semicolons if there is more than one. For a complete description of line-for-line style, see *The Chicago Manual*.

Alphabetizing Main Entries. Use the letter-by-letter method, which ignores spaces and punctuation up to the first comma. Alphabetize numbers and symbols as if they were spelled out. Use inversion to make the most important word come first. See *The Chicago Manual* for an extensive discussion of alphabetization.

Grammar of Main Entries. Every main entry must be a noun in some form. It may be a common or proper noun, such as *Evaluation;* a gerund such as *Evaluating;* or a noun phrase such as *Evaluating performance, Job evaluations*, and *Evaluation of performance*. Turn adjectives and verbs into noun phrases or gerunds.

Alphabetizing Subentries. Arrange subentries in alphabetical order by the first important word, called the **key word.** Ignore introductory prepositions and conjunctions, such as *and, by, for,* and *with*.

Grammar of Subentries. Subentries do not have to form a grammatical phrase with the main entry. Use prepositions and conjunctions when necessary to clarify the relationship between the main entry and subentry. The most important consideration is making sense to the reader.

Page References. Use inclusive page references that indicate where the discussion begins and ends, for example, 12–18. Do not use *f* and *ff*. Use full inclusive numbers, such as 135–138 (as opposed to 135–38).

The following example illustrates proper style, alphabetization, and grammar:

> New Mexico, 10–26
>   climate, 24
>   in folklore, 26
>   geography, 18–23
>   history, 11–17
>   *See also* Southwestern United States
> Newton, City of, 111–112
> Newton Art Association, The, 45
> New York. *See* Capital cities; Empire State Building
> *1984*, 55
> # (Number sign), 460

Submitting Index Manuscripts. Follow the general rules described in Chapter 6 of this guide. Double-space the index. Quadruple-space between letters of the alphabet. Begin main entries with a capital letter, and begin subentries with lowercase letters, unless otherwise indicated by the text. Indent each subentry by one tab. Put *See* and *See also* in italics. Do not format in multiple columns. Number manuscript pages in the upper-right-hand corner. If possible, provide a computer disk or electronic transmission along with hard copy.

PRINTED ENDPAPERS OR PRINTED INSIDE COVERS

On some books, like this *Author's Guide*, copy is printed on the inside of the covers. This feature is referred to as **printed endpapers** on hardcover books and as **printed inside covers** on paperback books. Consult your acquisitions editor about whether your book will have one of these features. Find out whether it will include both art and text, and whether copy will appear inside both the front and back covers. Submit copy for endpapers or inside covers along with the text and art manuscripts, prepare it according to the same guidelines, and clearly label it as endpaper or inside cover copy.

PREPARING THE ILLUSTRATIONS

An illustration program is much more than a decorative afterthought. An excellent art program can enhance pedagogy, motivate readers, and significantly increase your text's marketability and sales. Properly developing your art manuscript will help ensure the quality and accuracy of illustrations in the printed book.

It is important that a complete illustration manuscript accompany the first draft of your text, for two reasons: (1) we need clear, carefully labeled illustrations if we are to receive worthwhile feedback on the art program during the review process; (2) in books with extensive illustration programs, we may have to begin photo research and art production while text manuscript is still being revised in order that illustrations will be at least in progress when final text manuscript is turned over from Editorial to Production.

Review your text manuscript with a view toward how visuals might clarify important concepts. For each figure, ask yourself, "What is the most important point?" Then put yourself in the student's position and try to imagine how visuals might help you learn. You, the reader, should be able to review most key points in the chapter by reviewing the art. Also review the art programs of your main competitors. Do these texts contain standard diagrams or photos that you may have overlooked? Do you have new concepts or innovative visual ideas that will set your text apart from the competition? If you need help developing your ideas, try to assess the number of such figures and let your editor know the level of assistance you'll require. Send representative samples of your illustrations to your acquisitions or development editor. By letting us have an early look, we can work together to produce high-quality artwork and avoid costly problems and delays in production.

Like the text, illustrations go through several production stages before the book is printed. Initially, art and text travel on separate paths. While text files are edited, reviewed, and updated, illustrations go to an art studio for drafting or "rendering." Art and text must travel concurrently so that they can be combined in pages at the same time (see Chapter 10 for a discussion of proof stages).

Take the time develop your illustration manuscript properly. Your hard work will pay off!

TYPES OF ILLUSTRATIONS

An **illustration manuscript** may include the following categories of art: technical line art (including simple graphs and charts, cartoons, and maps), more complex three-dimensional or shaded art, and photographs. We will discuss each of these categories in detail. (Tables and other pedagogical devices such as boxes are key-boarded as part of the text and are not considered illustrations. Therefore, they should be submitted as part of the text manuscript.)

As you read on, keep in mind that art studios are generally *not* equipped to conceptualize or research your ideas, and it is best not to assume they have exper-tise in your field. It is the author's responsibility to communicate art concepts clearly and comprehensively by means of an **art sketch**—your best visual repre-sentation of a concept. If you don't feel your own sketch fully communicates your intent, you can append a few examples of similar figures (photocopies or tearsheets) from other sources as references. When supplying a drawing from another source, indicate whether it is to be matched as closely as possible or adapt-ed. When the figure is matched or adapted, you may need to obtain permission from the original source (see Chapter 5).

If you are using an illustration program (for example, Adobe Illustrator or Maple) to prepare your art, be sure to consult with your acquisitions or develop-ment editor, who will put you in touch with a staff person who can provide guide-lines for submission or evaluate your art early on.

LINE ART

Line art is a flat, two-dimensional figure drawn with lines (black or color) and per-haps filled in with tinted areas; the category includes graphs and charts, flow dia-grams, technical diagrams, maps, and cartoons.

Most technical art is rendered as line art because of the clarity with which complex detail can be depicted. Such illustrations require precise instructions for the artist, indicating when he or she must copy your sketch exactly and when slight variations are acceptable. Include information on perspective, level of detail, exact angles, and so on. For example, if an angle's value is critical, draw the angle accu-rately *and* indicate its value. (Circle the value if you don't want it to appear in the printed figure.) You may also need to specify if figure elements should be rendered in relative scale (for example, if one arrow should be twice as long as another or if one shape should be half as large as another).

Submit all graphs and charts in which accuracy is essential as computer-generated hard copy, or draw them on graph paper, inserting the coordinating points

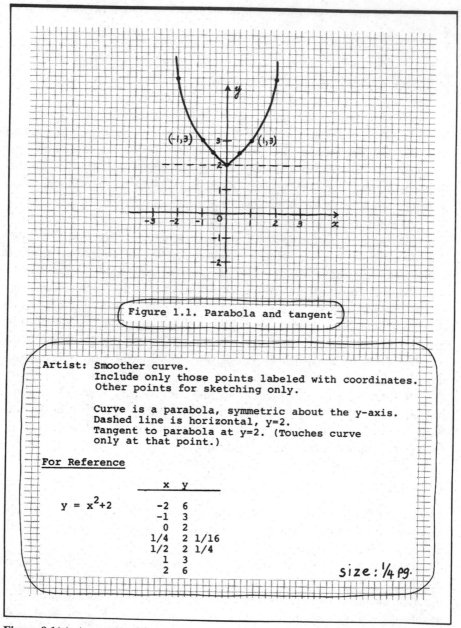

Figure 1.1. Parabola and tangent

Artist: Smoother curve.
Include only those points labeled with coordinates.
Other points for sketching only.

Curve is a parabola, symmetric about the y-axis.
Dashed line is horizontal, y=2.
Tangent to parabola at y=2. (Touches curve
only at that point.)

For Reference

$y = x^2+2$

x	y
-2	6
-1	3
0	2
1/4	2 1/16
1/2	2 1/4
1	3
2	6

size: 1/4 pg.

Figure 9.1(a) A properly prepared line art sketch submitted by an author.

and drawing the lines precisely. Whenever possible, provide up-to-date data. (Again, circle any values that you don't want to appear in the final figure.) Your goal is to provide clear, detailed, accurate sketches for every piece of art you submit. [See Figures 9.1(a) and (b).]

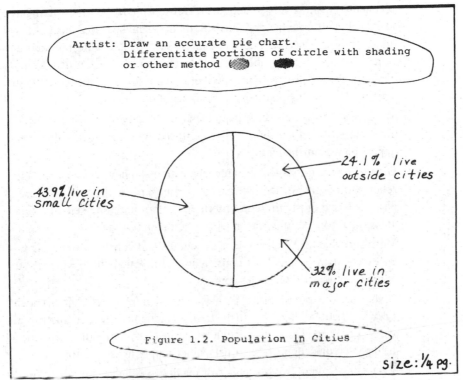

Artist: Draw an accurate pie chart.
        Differentiate portions of circle with shading
        or other method

24.1% live outside cities

43.9% live in small cities

32% live in major cities

Figure 1.2. Population in Cities

size: ¼ pg.

Figure 9.1(b) Another example of a properly prepared line art sketch.

THREE-DIMENSIONAL OR SHADED LINE ART

Three-dimensional line art may be black and white or color; it may be drawn by hand or on a computer; it may rest on a plain background or be part of a detailed scene of the real world. Its identifying characteristic is *shadings* that give the figure a realistic, modeled appearance. Because of its realism and its complexity, this category of art is generally more expensive than simple line art.

When dealing with three-dimensional line art, illustrators are encouraged to be creative in their interpretation of authors' art sketches, because part of their job is to raise the quality of the illustration to a new level. Therefore, it is very important that the author's original sketch contain detailed instructions as to where colors, proportions, and details can and cannot be changed.

PREPARING LINE ART SKETCHES

Don't be intimidated by the thought of creating art sketches. Just follow these guidelines:

1. Place each illustration on a *separate* piece of standard-size paper. Do not put text and illustrations on the same page because, as described above,

text and art manuscripts sometimes travel separately. For a revision, paste tearsheet of art from the previous edition on a standard-size sheet of paper and specify any necessary corrections. Be sure to include the previous edition figure and page number so that the figure can be identified. Identify each sketch with its *new* figure number (see our discussion later in the section on "Numbering and Separating Illustrations").

2. Write neat, concise instructions to the artist directly on the sketch, but circle them so that they will not be confused with any labels that are to appear on the finished art.

3. Directly on the art sketch, provide suggestions on how to size each figure relative to the size of the text page: margin, ¼ page, ⅓ page, ½ page, full page. The two most common criteria for determining the size of a figure are its pedagogical importance and its complexity.

4. Make sure that all labels are clear, accurate, and consistent with the text. Be especially vigilant about consistency with your book if you are submitting references from other sources.

5. If your art program consists of a variety of graphs and charts, indicate whether a grid should appear in the finished drawing. When accuracy is critical, you may need to attach specific numerical data for plotting. Provide all the data that must appear; the artist cannot supply missing information.

6. If you use stippling, cross-hatching, or shading to delineate portions of drawings or diagrams, be consistent in their use from one figure to another.

7. If your book is to be printed in multiple colors, indicate which elements in each line drawing would benefit from a functional use of color. Use color consistently throughout. We prefer that you place your instructions directly on the sketch in language simple enough for a layperson to understand; that is, use no technical jargon.

8. If you're attaching reference material to a sketch, be sure to mark the attached material "for reference only." If you submit more than one reference, clearly indicate what you want from each one (for example, the perspective on one, the detail on another, the style of arrows and brackets on another), but be sure that the content and labels you want are reflected on one "master sketch." (The artist is not responsible for knowing how to combine or condense illustrations from several sketches without instructions from you.)

Before the book is printed, you will receive illustration proofs, complete with labels. This will be your final opportunity to review rendered art. (See Figure 9.2 for examples of finished art that will be sent to you for checking.) You should review these proofs thoroughly, making sure that they are absolutely accurate and that they correspond to text discussions. All changes to illustrations must be made

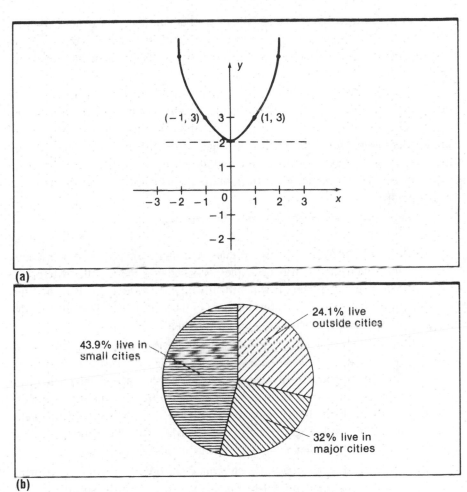

(a)

(b)

Figure 9.2 Finished versions of (a) Figure 9.1(a) and (b) Figure 9.1(b).

at this time. We will check revised proofs in house to ensure that all your changes have been incorporated. It is especially important to check label copy and the sizing of the art, as figure sizes should not be altered once the book has been paged.

PHOTOGRAPHS

Photographs are frequently used for their clear, realistic representation of the world. They must be carefully chosen for sharp focus and good contrast between light and dark areas. We prefer to use professional-quality images—either 5×7 or 8×10 black-and-white glossy prints or 35 mm four-color slides. High-quality color *prints* can also be scanned for reproduction, but they tend to lose a little more quality in the process. When selecting photographs, keep in mind that all images tend to lose some of their sharpness and to darken in tone when printed.

If you have accepted responsibility for obtaining the photographs for your book, be sure to consider the age, sex, race, and ethnicity of people shown in photos and aim for a representative mix. Be alert to styles, fashions, and hairdos shown in the images; avoid photos that look dated.

If you supply photos that have been published before or that were provided by an outside source, you need to obtain a formal permissions agreement from the copyright holder. (See Chapter 5 for more information on permissions.) Generally, permission for photographs is granted for one-time use only. If you are preparing a revised edition, you will probably have to reobtain permissions. Check the permissions file from the previous edition to verify the usage rights granted.

Follow these guidelines when submitting photographs:

1. Photos, slides, and cartoon prints are easily damaged. Avoid fastening them with paper clips or staples or smudging them with fingerprints. When shipping them, cushion them with cardboard and elastic, and further protect slides by inserting them in the clear plastic sleeves available in photo stores. (See Chapter 6 for shipping instructions.)

2. Write or type the figure number of the photograph (that is, the figure number that will appear in the book) on a gummed label and attach it to the back of the photograph. (Writing directly on the back of the photo could leave an impression that will be visible on the front.) Even if photographs aren't numbered in the book, they must have working identification numbers (Photo 1.1, 1.2, 1.3, and so on) consistent with the working numbers used to identify their captions and text call outs.

3. Make three photocopies of each print. One copy is for your files; submit two with the actual print. Use the photocopies to indicate specific instructions, such as **cropping** or special labels. (Cropping is a means to indicate that only a certain portion of the photo is to be used.) As with other art, you may also indicate a size preference: small, medium, or large. If appropriate, indicate the top and bottom of the image.

4. If your book includes color photographs, provide 35 mm transparencies (slides). Write the figure number on the cardboard border and put the slide in a plastic holder or a small envelope on which the figure number has been written as well. Write instructions for top/bottom and cropping on the cardboard. For every transparency, you should provide a working print or a full-size photocopy, with the figure number, labels, and crop marks clearly specified.

5. If color slides will eventually appear as black-and-white text images, please supply reproduction-quality black-and-white conversions made by

a reputable photo lab. Again, submit photocopies of each, marked with special instructions, labels, and so forth. Keep a copy for your files.

6. In some cases, people appearing in photos must sign model releases. For further information, consult *Photography and the Law* by Christopher Du Vernet.

7. If the photographs you supply are your own or are in the public domain, only a source note is required. However, if photographs come from another source or publication, you must arrange a formal permissions agreement. (For more information, contact Addison-Wesley's Rights and Permissions Department.) Check the other publication for the original source and copyright year. When appropriate, provide the photographer's full name and/or the stock agency that supplied the photo, along with the address. Add these to your caption manuscript (see Chapter 7). The source could also be a museum, library, colleague, or government agency.

8. Advertisements and composite photos have special permissions needs. Consult your acquisitions or development editor if you plan to use this type of material.

9. If you wish to use any photographs or line art from an existing Addison Wesley Longman title, see Chapter 13 for instructions.

If you're unable to provide photographs for your text, talk to your acquisitions editor or project manager about having Addison-Wesley assist you with photo research. Because this service can be time-consuming and expensive, it is generally covered in a contractual agreement. Discuss this matter with your editor early in the writing process. You will be asked to provide a photo specification list that includes instructions about the point you want each photo to make. For example, instead of saying "woman in an office," specify "woman about 30 to 40 talking to colleagues at work. Woman should look animated and persuasive as though she were pitching a new idea." Your selections need to be finalized before your manuscript is released to production, so be sure to allow time for the research and securement of the right images. Discuss the schedule with your editor.

CARTOONS

Although we discuss cartoons here as a separate category of illustration, they should be submitted in the form of camera-ready art (see below). Good-quality tearsheets from magazines can be scanned and are acceptable for reproduction; however, clippings from newspapers are unacceptable. Preferably, you should write to the original source, requesting both permission to use the cartoon and a glossy 8×10-inch, black-and-white print for reproduction. Follow the same guidelines for handling and shipping cartoons as those given for photographs (see the previous section on "Photographs" and Chapter 6).

MAPS

When submitting map manuscript to be drawn, follow the same guidelines given earlier in this chapter for preparing line art sketches. In addition, do the following:

1. If possible, provide tearsheets or clear photocopies of maps. Otherwise, use large outline maps or accurate tracings as the basis for your sketches. Indicate the scale you have used, the exact area the map is to cover, and any special projection you want. Supply examples of map styles and palettes you like.

2. Include *all labels in place on the sketch*—countries, provinces, cities, mountains, rivers, oceans, and so on. Review labels carefully, checking for consistency with the text and map caption.

3. When submitting tearsheets, edit out labels and any details that should not appear on your map.

4. Specify any internal borders and geographical features that should be depicted. If the map is being rendered by a cartographic studio, the artist will generally update boundaries and country names.

5. Indicate special areas to be highlighted. The artist can choose the color or shading but generally cannot make pedagogical decisions about which features to show or emphasize.

CAMERA-READY ART

Camera-ready art is black-and-white artwork (other than photographs) that is ready to be scanned for reproduction without further work—other than minor cropping or size reduction. This kind of art does not go to a studio for rendering. Some examples of camera-ready art are printed forms, stock quotes, computer printouts, and cartoons.

Because you must submit copy that is suitable for reproduction, it should be very clear with good contrast, and it should not be bent or damaged in any way. You should follow the same guidelines for handling and shipping camera-ready art as those given for photographs (see the previous section on "Photographs" and Chapter 6).

If camera-ready art cannot be reduced (this is the case, for example, with some computer printouts), then be sure to find out the text width from your acquisitions editor before preparing the material.

NUMBERING AND SEPARATING ILLUSTRATIONS

Each figure in your art manuscript should occupy a single sheet of white paper, with all figures gathered together at the end of each chapter. Use a double-numbering system to identify all figures that will be numbered in the final work. Please number figures consecutively within chapters, beginning with number 1 for the first figure in each chapter. That is, in Chapter 3, start with Figure 3.1, Figure 3.2, and so on, until you reach the last figure; then start your numbering again in Chapter 4 with Figure 4.1, Figure 4.2, and so on.

Always refer to figures by number in the text. Your reference to the figure number will indicate approximately where the illustration should be positioned. Call-outs for figures should appear in parentheses at the end of the paragraph in which the figure is referenced. If the figure is unnumbered, please indicate between text paragraphs approximately where you would like it to appear. Unnumbered figures must still have working numbers for identification. Identify them by both chapter number and an AIT (art in text) designation, for example, AIT 1.1, AIT 2.3, and so on).

Remember, you must provide a complete illustration manuscript *separate from the text manuscript*. Place each illustration on a separate page; no manuscript page should contain both art and text. For photographs, camera-ready art, and cartoons, include photocopies in the illustration manuscript, while keeping the original material carefully and separately packaged. Your acquisitions or development editor will provide you with an **art log** to help you keep track of all artwork. Please submit your art log along with each draft of manuscript. Art logs are now available in electronic form as well as hard copy; request a disk from your acquisitions editor.

Preparing Captions

Most figures—with the exception of AITs—should be accompanied by a caption (or legend). **Captions** are brief descriptions of each figure, and they should include credit lines where appropriate. (See the discussion in Chapter 7 on "Captions.") Unless otherwise instructed, do not include captions in the text body or on the art sketches. The latter will only confuse studio artists because, although captions appear with their corresponding illustrations in the printed book, they travel separately from illustrations during early stages of production. Copyeditors are editing and correcting captions at the same time that art studios are sizing and rendering illustrations. You should place captions for each chapter at the end of the text manuscript for that chapter, after any end-of-chapter text elements such as questions, or a bibliography.

Storing Illustrations

Contemporary graphic artists prepare art electronically by computer, with the final product stored on a disk. Art prepared on disks will be stored at Addison Wesley Longman for use in subsequent editions or for reprint corrections.

Producing the Book

Your work is not over with the submission of your final manuscript. Your production supervisor reviews the manuscript for completeness before it begins moving through the production and manufacturing stages. As we mentioned earlier, you play an important role in what happens next.

Addison Wesley Longman has always stayed on the cutting edge of using the latest technologies to support authors and produce textbooks. Our goal, therefore, is to have a digitized reusable end product that might be used for the creation of future revisions of your book or for the customization of your book. Therefore, we prefer to receive your manuscript in a consistently prepared, word-processed format (see Chapter 6 for further details concerning manuscript preparation). Digitizing the content of your manuscript will allow us to accomplish a number of objectives—specifically, to:

- Take advantage of the technologies now available
- Streamline the process and publish more accurate books
- Make better use of your time during the production process
- Permit archiving of all text and graphics files, easing the creation of custom books and allowing us to generate files, when appropriate, for you to use in preparing future editions.

Your cooperation during the production process is essential to the timely publication of an accurate text. The process begins with the turnover of a complete, well-prepared final manuscript.

Stages in the Production Process

The **production process** refers to the stages your manuscript goes through before it becomes a bound book. A production supervisor will be assigned to your book and will be your primary contact throughout the process. He or she will guide you through each production stage and give you scheduling information. However, the production supervisor is only one part of an informed team of people (both inside and freelance) working to publish your text, some of whom may contact you during the production cycle. Schedules are critical at this point in the publication process. If you anticipate difficulty in meeting any of your deadlines, or if you are planning vacation time during the production process, let your production supervisor know at once.

The following is a brief description of the production stages. The rest of the chapter is devoted to discussing these stages in more detail.

- A production supervisor evaluates the manuscript's design and copyediting needs.
- The text and cover design process begins.
- Text manuscript, including front matter and back matter, and line art manuscript go to a copyeditor for editing
- The author and the production supervisor review the copyedited manuscript.
- Illustrations go to the art studio for rendering (for texts with extensive illustration programs, this process may have started before turnover of final manuscript).
- Illustration proofs are checked by the author and returned to the art studio for corrections.
- The edited text manuscript goes to a compositor, who updates author-supplied disks by entering edits to the files or who rekeys the manuscript if files are not available.
- The final art is released for processing and incorporating into the first page proof stage.
- Text and art files go to the compositor for electronic page makeup.
- The author, the production supervisor, and sometimes the development editor review the first-pass pages while a proofreader simultaneously proofreads against the manuscript.
- Work on the index manuscript begins.
- The first-pass page proofs are returned for corrections.
- Final pages are checked by the production department. (Authors of books with heavy math or other highly technical material routinely review both sets of pages, and often these reviews are correlated with the work of accuracy checkers.)
- Final disks are sent to a film output source or directly to the printer.
- Blues (film proofs) are provided by the printer for an in-house check.
- Covers and endpapers (if applicable) are printed and shipped to the binder.
- Books are printed, bound, and shipped to the warehouse.

TEXT DESIGN AND COVER DESIGN

Once your manuscript is in the hands of our production staff, your production supervisor will identify every text element so that the interior text design can begin. As soon as we have examples of all text elements, we can begin the design process, which often occurs before final manuscript is complete. Text elements include chapter titles, headings, captions, tables, end-of-chapter summaries, and so forth. Your acquisitions editor and/or development editor and production supervisor will work with a professional designer who will design these elements. Once a final design is approved, the compositor will begin formatting the copyedited manuscript, and the art studio will begin rendering the line art. In addition, the complete front matter manuscript will be prepared for design. Since any changes after this point will be costly, it is important that you communicate any special requirements or restrictions involving the text design to your acquisitions or development editor when you submit your final manuscript.

Planning for the cover begins early in the production process. The acquisitions editor, development editor, and marketing manager confer with the designer to determine the type of cover that will best appeal to the market and enhance the text. A designer conceptualizes the design for the cover, which begins its production stages shortly after the text.

COPYEDITING

One of the first stages in the production process is **copyediting**—getting the text into polished grammatical and stylistic shape. This stage is supervised by the production supervisor. As discussed previously, our primary reference sources for spelling, punctuation, and grammar are the latest editions of *Webster's New Collegiate Dictionary* and *The Chicago Manual of Style*. The production supervisor or the copyeditor will send you a copy of the style sheet or a sample chapter or two for your approval prior to copyediting.

The **copyeditor** works on the assumption that the substance of the text is accurate. You are responsible for the content, the correctness of figures and dates, the accuracy with which any quotations are reproduced, and the correct citation of sources. It is the copyeditor's job to check the mechanical details of writing, including spelling, punctuation, and grammar; to catch inconsistencies of style and form; and to mark design codes on the manuscript for the compositor. The copyeditor will also question you if your meaning is not clear, will make minor changes to improve expression and structure, and will ask you to supply missing information.

After the manuscript has been copyedited, the production supervisor will send it to you for review. (He or she reviews it as well.) You will receive the copyedited art manuscript along with the copyedited text manuscript, or sometimes prior to the text, so that the art rendering can proceed while you are reviewing the text manuscript. Getting an early jump on preparing the art allows for art proofs to be ready at the same time as the text manuscript to go to pages. You must check every detail in reviewing the editing. When you return the manuscript, you imply acceptance of it as it now stands. This is your last opportunity to make changes without incurring additional expense. Changes made in proof stages can be costly and time-consuming. (See the section on "Author's Alterations" later in the chapter.)

PROOFS

Proofs are duplicate copies of electronically composed material and artwork; they are used as a vehicle for reviewing text and art and correcting errors before printing. You will be involved with checking one or two proof stages—the first-pass pages and perhaps the second-pass pages. Your production supervisor will send you a preliminary production schedule before you begin and will let you know if there are any scheduling changes.

Illustration Proofs. You will be sent **illustration proofs** (photocopies of finished line art for the newly drawn artwork in your book), along with your original copyedited art sketches, usually in advance of the related text material so that the illustration proofs will be ready to be combined with the text in the paging stage (see the following section). Carefully examine each piece of art, making sure that all labels are correctly spelled and properly positioned and that each drawing has been correctly interpreted; please check all leaders (lines extending from a label to the appropriate part of a line illustration or photograph) at this stage as well. For texts printed in more than one color, composite color or color-separated proofs will be provided; these "laser proofs" indicate how color is used in the illustrations, but the color shown will not exactly match the final printed color; it is merely representative. Note corrections directly on the art proofs, and return all materials by the scheduled due date.

First-Pass Pages. The first stage of your text during composition is **page proofs**. With the exception of the index, you will receive a complete set of proofs for the entire text, usually sent in batches of chapters by your production supervisor. Make all of your corrections on one copy and then make a copy, which you should keep for your reference in the preparation of the index. Be sure to mark your corrections on the original very neatly.

Although a professional proofreader will read these page proofs against the manuscript for typographical errors ("typos") at the same time you are reading them, you are responsible for reading this first proof stage very carefully. There may be errors that a proofreader—who generally does not have your expertise in the subject matter—may miss. Read every letter, punctuation mark, and space. Look for typos, spelling errors, inconsistent usage, and content errors. See the inside front and back covers of this guide for proofreading symbols and for the conventional way to mark proofs.

Remember that since corrections in proofs are expensive and can affect the schedule, they should be kept to a minimum. (We will discuss these corrections, known as author's alterations, in greater detail later in the chapter.)

You must also answer all **author queries** that appear on the proofs. These are unresolved questions that only you can answer. Missing cross-references will have to be supplied by you. Queries regarding design (for example, spacing, type size, arrangement of material) will be resolved by the designer after you return proofs.

Once you return the page proofs, the production supervisor will transfer your corrections to the proofreader's set of pages, check all notations, and ensure that all queries are answered before returning the page proofs to the compositor for correction. Your index manuscript is due shortly after you return the last batch of page proofs.

Second-Pass Pages. After the first-pass pages, the compositor sends one more proof stage to us for a quality check. We ensure that all corrections requested in page proofs have been made, that no new errors have been introduced, and that all material is correct and in place. In most cases, you will be consulted only if some content questions arise or artwork was not in place in first-pass page proofs. Authors preparing their own index will receive a copy of the second-pass pages for confirmation purposes.

This final page proof stage is released in the form of files or film to the printer. But before the book actually goes on press, the printer sends "blues" to us for review. A proof of the final output, blues are our final look at the entire book before it is printed and bound.

AUTHOR'S ALTERATIONS (AAs)

One of the primary concerns of authors and publishers is to produce books with as few errors as possible. Following the guidelines given in this *Author's Guide* for preparing text and art manuscripts will help ensure the accuracy of your book. Careful checking of copyedited text manuscript and of text and illustration proofs is essential as well if we are to achieve our common goal of publishing an excellent textbook.

Corrections in text and illustration proofs are expensive and can adversely affect the schedule, so you should make any necessary changes as early as possible in the process, preferably when you review your copyedited manuscript. (No charges are incurred for corrections to copyedited manuscript.) Because it is likely, however, that some refinements will still be needed after copyediting, it is important for you to understand our author's alterations policy.

AUTHOR'S ALTERATIONS IN TEXT

An **author's alteration** in text (in publishing terms, an **AA**) is any change in proofs other than the correction of an error introduced by the compositor. All AAs are charged to the publisher by the compositor. **Compositor errors** (formerly printer's errors and therefore called **PEs**) are mistakes made by the compositor during the initial keyboarding of your manuscript or while making changes in proof stages. Compositor errors are not charged to the publisher; however, if a compositor error goes unnoticed when it is first introduced and is caught at a later stage by you, the proofreader, or the production supervisor, it is considered an AA and charged to the publisher. Even though changes that you, the production supervisor, or the proof-reader make may be necessary—to ensure consistency, to add credit lines, or to insert page cross-references—they are still all classified as author's alterations.

Proof corrections may be thought of as "repairs," and repair work is always expensive. At each successive proof stage, the expense and difficulty increase. In first-pass pages, for example, the addition or deletion of lines may involve rerunning not simply a few lines but an entire chapter! That is why the proper preparation of your text manuscript and your thorough check of copyedited manuscript are so important.

AUTHOR'S ALTERATIONS IN ART

Corrections made on illustrations that we draw for your book are categorized and charged in a manner similar to text corrections. An author's alteration in art is any change in illustration proofs other than the correction of an error introduced by the art studio. Because our schedules do not always allow for you to review copyedited art manuscript, it is essential that the art manuscript you submit initially be accurate and complete and that you adhere to our instructions regarding art. As with text changes, making numerous corrections after illustrations have been drawn can be extremely expensive. The later in the process that art corrections are made, the more costly and involved they become. Correcting art at the page proof stage, for example, is prohibitively expensive. Not only does the art correction have to be made by the studio, but the art must be removed from the page and a new, corrected version substituted.

AUTHOR'S ALTERATION ALLOWANCE

The author's alteration allowance, as stated in your contract, is a percentage of the original cost of composition and art rendering for your textbook. Addison Wesley Longman will absorb the cost of all author's alterations that fall within that specified allowance, but alteration costs in excess of your allowance are charged against your royalties. Although it is often difficult to gauge exactly when you are at the point of exceeding your AA allowance, we will alert you if we feel that there is a danger that you will go beyond the limit. The best advice for staying within your allowance is to take care of as many problems as possible in the manuscript stage (where changes are free), to make any necessary changes in the earliest proof stage possible, and to keep all corrections to a minimum. Most important, a carefully prepared manuscript is your best insurance against incurring excess author's alteration charges.

REPRINT CORRECTIONS

No matter how thorough you and the proofreaders have been, small errors are sometimes missed and appear in the printed book. Around the time that the book is published, you will receive instructions to correct these errors on tearsheets or on photocopies of book pages. These corrections should be forwarded to your acquisitions or development editor. Corrections are usually made only to the first reprint of the text, so a careful review of your published book is critical.

A reprint may be scheduled quickly and with short notice, so getting these corrections to us right away will ensure their inclusion in the second printing (the first reprint). **Reprint corrections** should not be made on the basis of style or aesthetics. Their sole purpose is to correct erroneous content or any mistake involving credits or permissions that could result in legal action.

Developing the Supplements

You may be the author of not just a text but of a complete textbook package, containing a text and a variety of supporting supplements. In our most competitive markets, supplements are far from luxuries that we can decide to publish or not. On the contrary, they often determine the ultimate success of a book, and they are a crucial element in many adoption decisions. Ancillary materials are more and more becoming central components of an entire teaching and learning program.

Because supplements should be published at the same time as the text itself, the development and writing should begin as early as possible. Make a point of discussing plans for all supplements with your acquisitions editor as soon as your publishing contract is signed. Specifically, analyze the length and content of each supplement and determine with the acquisitions editor whether you will write certain supplements, or if we will need to hire additional authors. Your suggestions for supplements authors are greatly appreciated. Once we have signed authors for each supplement, we may call on you to review samples of their work. It is of the utmost importance that the entire program reflect your voice and the vision presented in your book. Therefore, your participation and involvement in the supplements package are crucial. By giving the same care and attention to the ancillaries that you have devoted to your text, you can count on an effective, tightly integrated program that will contribute to increased sales of your textbook.

Writing Your Own Supplements

If you are writing your own supplements, you may feel a bit daunted at first. Getting the work on the ancillaries done along with that of the textbook may be a juggling act, but do not panic. Your editor will work closely with you and guide you through the process of creating your supplements from start to finish. He or she will provide you with a copy of our *Instructions for Creating Camera-Ready Copy*, complete step-by-step guidelines for formatting professional-looking, final camera-ready copy, and will help you coordinate your writing schedule as well as traffic the proofreading, copyediting, and reviewing of the supplements.

As you write the individual text chapters, it is a good idea to make notes to yourself about items or ideas that might be used in the supplements. Some of your best ideas will occur to you as you write the text; do not assume that you will remember them later. Keeping notes is especially important if you are supplying solutions to end-of-chapter questions or problems that will go into the instructor's manual. If you do not write the answers or solutions at the same time that you create these items, you may have trouble reconstructing them later. Similarly, if you are writing the test bank, it is best to create questions and answers simultaneously with writing the main text.

THE MOST COMMON TEXT SUPPLEMENTS

The most widely used text supplements include instructor's manuals, test banks, study guides, answer manuals, solutions manuals, transparencies, and specialized electronic supplements such as data disks, PowerPoint presentations, and computerized test banks.

INSTRUCTOR'S MANUAL, INSTRUCTOR'S SOLUTIONS MANUAL, INSTRUCTORS RESOURCE GUIDE

Perhaps the most crucial item in the supplements package is the **instructor's manual**. A well-written instructor's manual with the right mix of features can be a powerful inducement to instructors to adopt your book. Features may include:

1. Alternative approaches to presenting or sequencing chapter content
2. Hints on adapting the text to shorter courses or ones with specialized aims
3. Sample syllabi for 10- and 14-week courses
4. Chapter synopses in narrative form, in which the author summarizes a chapter's content and briefly explains the chapter's focus
5. Chapter outlines
6. Lists of key terms
7. Teaching hints, drawn from the author's personal experiences, that provide additional ideas or examples
8. Suggested exercises or class projects
9. Answers to the end-of-chapter questions or cases that appear in the text
10. Solutions to text exercises (see "Solutions Manual," below)
11. Additional writing exercises, essay questions, or problems, along with suggested answers or solutions

12. Objective test items, such as multiple-choice or true-false questions with answers if there is no separate test bank

13. Selected bibliographies for each chapter

14. Answers to questions in the study guide, if one exists

15. Tips on course management and administration

As the one most familiar with the text's content and aims, you are the ideal author for the instructor's manual. Even if you decide to get help from someone else (sometimes time demands leave you no choice), supply such items as chapter-content reviews, teaching suggestions, and answers to end-of-chapter questions or problems yourself. You know this material better than anyone else, and your mastery of it will show in the writing.

Other kinds of instructor's manuals, including an instructor's solutions manual and instructor's resource guide, may be important for the market. Consult with your editor as to which form the instructor's manual should take.

Because the instructor's manual is given free of charge to instructors who adopt your book, it is critical that we publish it on schedule and within budget. We can do so only if you submit proofread **camera-ready copy** (we'll discuss the preparation of camera-ready copy later in the chapter).

TEST BANK (TEST ITEM FILE)

Test banks, also known as test item files, contain a battery of short questions and answers that instructors can use for their students. Test banks can be produced in electronic or printed form. An important part of many undergraduate text packages, accurate test banks are crucial to sales.

Questions in the test bank should be grouped by chapter, and each chapter should contain the same types of questions in the same proportion. The test questions within any question type should follow the order of presentation of topics within each chapter of your book. The best test items in the most professional testing supplements have been class tested and validated according to level of difficulty (easy, medium, difficult) and cognitive type (applied, interpretive, factual).

Test banks usually contain the following types of questions:

1. *Multiple-choice questions.* This is the preferred type of objective question in most disciplines. When in doubt, create more of these questions than any other type. Each should have four clear choices of answers. Avoid ambiguous answers such as "all of the above," "none of the above," or "both a and d." Indicate the correct answer by placing it on a separate line.

2. *True-false questions.* Indicate the correct answer by typing T or F in front of the statement.

3. *Fill-in-the-blank questions.* A blank is left so that the student can fill in the correct word or phrase. List the correct answers in a separate answer key.

4. *Short or long essay questions or problems.* Authors may provide typical essay answers, an outline of points to be covered in an essay, or calculations of a problem.

5. *Quizzes and tests.* Some test banks also include sample chapter quizzes or part quizzes, as well as sample midterm and final exams.

6. *Answer keys.* Some test banks may contain all of the answers in an answer key at the end of the chapter or the end of the supplement.

TESTGEN EQ

TestGen EQ, Addison-Wesley's computerized test generator, is available in Windows and Macintosh versions and is fully networkable. TestGen EQ's friendly, graphical interface enables instructors to view, edit, and add questions with ease; transfer questions to tests; and print tests in a variety of fonts and forms. Six question types are available, including short-answer, true-false, multiple-choice, essay, matching, and bimodal formats. A built-in question editor gives the user the power to create graphs, import graphics, insert mathematical symbols and templates, and insert variable numbers or text.

We strongly urge you to write your test bank in the TestGen EQ software program. Doing so will save time and money and will greatly minimize the possibility of errors in both the printed and computerized test banks. If you use TestGen EQ instead of submitting final camera-ready copy, you should send us final TestGen EQ data disks and a printout of your test items. We will then generate final camera-ready copy here for the printed version of the test bank. Author's manuals and program disks for TestGen EQ will be sent by your supplements editor or designated book team member.

STUDY GUIDE

A well-designed **study guide** gives students the opportunity to review important text concepts and to apply these concepts to questions and problems. Your study guide will not work unless it is easy to use. It should follow the same chapter sequence as the text, and the order of topics within chapters should also be the same.

Consider including the following features in each chapter of your study guide:

1. Learning objectives
2. Chapter overview (several paragraphs that tell students the main points of the chapter)
3. Chapter outline based on chapter headings
4. Key terms, sometimes defined

5. Essay questions, problems, or brief practice cases, often with answers provided

6. Programmed learning sections with blanks left for missing words or phrases (missing words are often supplied in right margins or elsewhere)

7. Matching exercises

8. Multiple-choice questions, with answers given at the end of the section or at the back of the guide

9. True-false questions, with answers given at the end of the section or at the back of the guide

10. Games, puzzles, or other activities

11. Additional projects

ANSWER BOOK AND SOLUTIONS MANUAL

Certain technical courses require an answer book or a solutions manual along with the text. An **answer book** contains the correct answers to specified text problems not already answered in the text. A **solutions manual** shows all the steps needed to work out designated text problems. Generally designed for the student's use, the latter typically takes the form of a **student solutions manual** that offers solutions to odd-numbered exercises from the text.

Again, it is best to develop these materials along with the text itself. The problems will be fresh in your mind, and you will not have the burden of providing all of the answers and solutions at once. To avoid inadvertent mistakes, your acquisitions editor may suggest an independent check of all problems and solutions. If this is required, sufficient time must be allowed in the production schedule.

TRANSPARENCIES

Many professors find the use of overhead **transparencies** very helpful in their teaching. A set of transparencies can consist of line illustrations and photographs from the text or supplemental key illustrative material. Reviewers of the first-draft and revised manuscript are sometimes asked which illustrations from the text might be helpful as transparencies; it will be easier to compose the final list if you make note of these suggestions as you go through the reviews.

POWERPOINT PRESENTATIONS

As classroom technology changes, more and more professors are turning to **PowerPoint slides** for course presentations. This specialized electronic supplement, which is broken up into chapters, may be one of many components of a CD-ROM. Black-and-white transparency masters are also sometimes produced from these presentations for insertion in the instructor's manual. Because art from the main text is usually used in these presentations, you may work with both the production coordinator and the supplements editor in developing this supplement. It is important that you consult with your acquisitions editor on the length, features, and version of PowerPoint to be used for the final presentation.

SPECIALIZED SUPPLEMENTS

In certain cases, personal computer software and other specialized supplements may accompany the text. The creation, testing, packaging, and manufacturing of supplements such as videos, laser discs, CD-ROMs, and computer software are a complex, highly individualized process handled by our media/software producers (see Chapter 1). Talk with your acquisitions editor if you believe that such material is appropriate for your text.

PREPARING CAMERA-READY COPY

As we mentioned earlier, we require that you provide camera-ready copy (copy that is ready for printing) for most print supplements. Creating this copy is your last step in the supplement preparation process. It comes after the material has been copyedited, the text cross-references supplied, and all artwork finalized. Your supplements editor or production coordinator will provide you with the aforementioned booklet, *Instructions for Creating Camera-Ready Copy*, to help you put together final copy for your supplements. It includes information on all aspects of preparing and producing text and art for supplements. Ask your supplements editor or production coordinator to send it to you if he or she has not already done so. You will probably be asked to supply some sample pages, based on the specifications outlined in the booklet, early on in the process to check that you are on the right track. In this way any problems can be corrected before the major work is under way.

COORDINATING TEXT AND SUPPLEMENTS SCHEDULES

To ensure that your supplements will be published on schedule with your text, you should provide final camera copy at least six to eight weeks prior to the text's bound book date. Be sure to talk to your supplements editor or production coordinator if a supplement has special design or editorial requirements (for example, ancillary materials such as CD-ROMs or user's guides that are packaged with the main text), because additional time may be required in order to publish it on schedule.

MARKETING AND SELLING THE BOOK

At Addison-Wesley, marketing is at the core of many of the strategic and tactical decisions we make, and our marketing process is concurrent and interwoven with the whole of the publishing process. Our marketing staff will work closely with you and with our editors to ensure that your book's strengths and distinctive features are readily evident in the published work as these are the foundation around which we will build our promotional and selling campaigns.

In the course of going through the publishing process as a team, you and your marketing manager will have already become close allies by the time of publication. You are both the colleague who best knows the product, and the friendly representative of the target market with firsthand knowledge of adoption criteria and market and discipline trends, as well as direct experience with the competition. Your willingness to engage actively with your marketing manager is a necessary first step in launching the promotional and selling campaigns that will help us win widespread endorsement and adoption of your work.

Another key step is the thoughtful completion of the Author's Questionnaire.

THE AUTHOR'S QUESTIONNAIRE

The **Author's Questionnaire (AQ)** is the document from which the marketing manager truly begins to build the marketing plan for your title. The AQ contains basic information, including the order of the authors' names, school affiliations, the complete book title, and more. It is also the primary means for you as the author to communicate your ideas for marketing your text.

The main categories in the AQ focus on:

- Personal information
- Product information
- Special features of your book
- The market
- Packaging
- Competition
- Conventions/exhibits
- Publicity
- Professional market opportunities

The marketing manager will review and use the information you provide for each of these categories in shaping the best possible plan for your book. Regardless of how often you and your marketing manager have spoken, it is important that you complete the AQ carefully as it is the base document that also serves our international and noncollege sales channels.

Specifically, this the ideal time for you to identify all potential markets for your title (in addition to its primary college market). If you believe that there are large prospective markets for your book in trade, international, professional, or other channels, this is the perfect opportunity for you to highlight these in the AQ in preparation for building the marketing plan. At the same time, if you have not already done so, it would be beneficial to begin preparing a list of prospective customers for your book. This list may comprise participants in a panel on which you also served, former students, research partners, professional acquaintances, representatives of companies for which you have offered consulting services, and more. Regardless of the size of the list, we will act upon each viable customer lead by bringing the customer's name to the attention of the sales staff most capable of following up on this sales opportunity.

Academic journals provide free publicity and have the endorsement of your peers. By using the AQ to identify those publications most likely to be read by prospective customers, you give us the information we need to provide their editors with prepublication copies of the manuscript and to ensure the timely publication of a review in a forthcoming edition. The "word-of-mouth" publicity can then be widespread by the time your book is published and ready for purchase.

MARKETING STRATEGY AND THE MARKETING PLAN

Marketing planning meetings are held in the year preceding your book's publication. During this time your marketing manager meets with representatives from various sales channels, with your editors, and with our convention planners, to discuss specific selling and promotional strategies for your work. Over the subsequent months your marketing manager will work closely with you and others to develop an individually tailored marketing plan that will address the potential sales of your book across all viable sales channels. In some instances we may elect to create cluster marketing plans or discipline catalogs to reach certain audiences more effectively.

A typical marketing plan includes the following categories:

- Basic information: title, sales estimate, price, bound book date, supplements
- Mission statement
- Market dynamics
- Product position/hallmark features
- The <your book> difference
- Competitive landscape (includes a brief analysis of the leading competitors' strengths and weaknesses)
- Issues for discussion
- Campaign concept/message
- Planned sales support
- Advertising timeline
- Conventions

SALES TOOLS

One of your marketing manager's most important responsibilities is the creation of the sales tools that our sales representatives will use when they present your book to potential customers. These materials are ultimately customized into situation-specific product kits, whether for presentations before a large text adoption committee or for appeals to "individual-choice" decision makers.

TABBING GUIDES

Tabbing guides are commonly used to direct prospective adopters to outstanding examples of your book's coverage and pedagogical apparatus. They are designed to structure a "walk-through" of your book and its accompanying set of supplementary teaching and learning aids. Tabbing guides come in a variety of formats and are employed in nearly every selling situation.

COMPETITIVE INFORMATION

At the core of successful strategy is specificity, and just as specific customer needs lead us to create correspondingly specific and satisfying product attributes, so does the selling process pit us head-to-head against specific competitors. Your marketing manager will be responsible for collecting, organizing, and disseminating information that most favorably compares and contrasts your book with the leading competitors.

Our authors are some of the best sources of this type of competitive information. Chances are that you have personally evaluated many of the leading textbooks over the years and have gone through the process of selecting one or more of them for adoption. You may even have direct classroom experience with some of these competing textbooks. For this reason we encourage our authors to remain current with respect to other textbooks on the market and to play an active role in the creation of competitor-specific selling tools.

PRODUCT INFORMATION RESOURCE LIBRARY (PIRL)

All our sales tools are formatted for storage and retrieval from PIRL, our intranet-accessible collection of selling tools that our sales representatives can download and customize for situation-specific use. Depending on the situation, a variety of other sales tools may be created to support the sales of your work. In each instance, you and your marketing manager will collaborate in this process.

NATIONAL AND REGIONAL SALES MEETINGS

Your book will be presented to our sales forces at several sales meetings, depending upon its publication date and the respective sales organizations that will bear greatest responsibility for selling the work. Addison Wesley Longman's Higher Education Publishing Group typically holds two national meetings and one regional meeting each year.

AUGUST NATIONAL SALES MEETING

The August National Sales Meeting is designed to highlight those titles with the greatest potential for adoptions in the forthcoming winter semester. In some instances, authors are invited to attend this meeting to assist with presenting their book. Presentations typically include an overview of the market, identification of distinctive product features, a "walk-through" of the book if appropriate, and competitive information.

JANUARY NATIONAL SALES MEETING

The January National Sales Meeting is more strategic and more specific in nature. Here, the sales representatives are expected to come to the meeting having conducted numerous interviews on the current copyright year's titles. They already understand the product features, and the purpose is to focus on winning the adoption, beating the competition, and reviewing "war stories" related to successful adoptions. Books published after the winter semester commences will be presented in January for the first time in a format similar to that of the August meeting.

REGIONAL MEETINGS

Spring regional meetings are run by the regional vice president of sales in conjunction with his or her sales management team. These meetings focus on identifying region-specific opportunities and maximizing sales. In-depth competitive information is reviewed, tactics are discussed, and newly revised titles to be published prior to the start of the fall semester are briefly introduced.

CHANNEL NATIONAL AND REGIONAL SALES MEETINGS

In addition to these sales meetings organized by the Higher Education Publishing Group, your marketing manager will coordinate appropriate communication with his or her counterparts in the International, School, Agency, Retail, and Corporate & Professional divisions to ensure that they have the information and tools necessary to exploit the sales of your book through their channels.

CONVENTIONS

Other publishers view conventions as an opportunity to showcase their titles in a given discipline. They bring cartons of books to display and then stand back, trusting that the right decision makers will enter the exhibition hall, hoping that the faculty members will visit their booths, and praying that the decision makers will have a few moments to browse their displays and complete an examination copy request form.

At Addison-Wesley, we believe that one should not pray for success; one should instead plan for success! Thus, every year we review the goals for each discipline and make decisions regarding our convention schedule according to our objectives for that given year. We then reflect on the primary product we have to offer for that year, and on the customers whom we are most determined to reach. We use this information to set in motion a plan to attract those customers. Our convention strategies for each year determine the type and size of booth, the selection of and number of text copies, and the personnel who will staff the booth.

WORKSHOPS

Addison-Wesley is privileged to enjoy a market-leading position in many of the disciplines for which we publish. Our authors are gifted thinkers and teachers. These advantages allow us to offer a unique series of workshops for selected markets, in which new teaching paradigms are shared, new technologies are introduced, and strategic partnerships are announced. The workshops are offered primarily as a service to faculty, with Addison-Wesley products used as reference points and with available titles on display for viewing during breaks. No "hard-sell" approach is attempted, nor would such an approach be tolerated. Feedback from the workshops is carefully evaluated in considering future endeavors.

ADVERTISING AND PROMOTIONAL MAILINGS

The most effective component of the promotional and selling process is the book itself. Accordingly, our advertising brochures and direct-mailing efforts are primarily geared toward identifying target customers and prompting them to request an examination copy of the book. Our challenge is one of optimization: how to maximize the total number of customers reviewing your book for possible adoption while at the same time efficiently sustaining interest in your book among those instructors who are most likely to adopt it for their classes.

With these goals in mind, we base our promotional campaigns on determining the customer behaviors we most want to influence and then on crafting the right message that will drive the desired behavior. Our advertising mailers come in a variety of forms and formats, including catalogs, cluster brochures, flip sheets, customized letters, and innovative folds and die-cut pieces.

TECHNOLOGY

The role of technology in product development, in the classroom, and in marketing continues to evolve in ever new and exciting ways. At Addison-Wesley we are rapidly adding to our electronic commerce capacity, and we welcome our authors' creative ideas on the use of technology in the marketing and selling of their texts and supplements.

THE WORLD WIDE WEB

Addison-Wesley maintains attractive World Wide Web sites for each discipline in which we publish. These sites may include cover shots, tables of contents, descriptions of pedagogical features, details on the supplements program, author information, and more. Some of our Web sites also include hyperlinks to other sites, provide information about the services we offer (such as workshops), and may offer specific interactive opportunities (such as projects, updates, and activities) for students and/or faculty.

LIVE CHATS

Students and faculty relish the opportunity to interact with textbook authors. Therefore, we will occasionally schedule "live chat" sessions on the Internet so that our authors can be available to interact with their various customers. An author's willingness to participate in these chats is critical to their success.

ADDITIONAL MARKETING IDEAS

As mentioned above, every title is unique, and for this reason we must evaluate the market opportunity for each title in an individual manner. There are some ways in which authors can truly make a difference in increasing the sales for their titles.

AUTHOR INVOLVEMENT

Some authors consider their role complete once the final manuscript is accepted for publication. To step back at this point is to miss an incredible ride! There are still so many ways in which you can partner with us to increase the visibility and likely success of your book. Some of these include your involvement at sales meetings, willingness to send a letter of introduction and encouragement to the sales force, and interest in participating in our e-mail and voice-mail systems. We also value your willingness to visit campuses where your book is a likely candidate for adoption. In addition, if you have any forthcoming speaking engagements, whether on campus or with professional organizations, we are happy to provide you with flyers to distribute to attendees who may elect to purchase copies of your book.

SELL-THROUGH

Once your book has been available for more than a semester, the most visible threat to its future success is the used-book market. Used-book distributors use sophisticated systems to ship inventory quickly from site to site and offer pricing incentives to students. Addison-Wesley will partner with you to fight this threat through a variety of means. During product development and the shaping of the marketing plan, we will brainstorm about possible means of limiting the used-book menace. Strategies include shrink-wrapping some product with your book (adding value), creating a value edition (pricing your new book similarly to a used book), and publishing an updated edition (increasing the value of your book through the addition of current information). Your help and creativity in developing these initiatives are always welcome.

REVISING THE TEXT FOR FUTURE EDITIONS

Now that you have brought your book to successful publication, you can rest—at least for a while. If book sales are strong, it is likely that we will ask you to revise the present edition. Although you will not have to start from scratch, you will need plenty of time for your revision work. And we will require the same amount of production time that it took during the last go-around to turn your manuscript into a bound book.

Thus, to get your book into production by a certain date, you and your acquisitions or development editor will have to plan carefully. That means starting the revision process early—usually a year before the completed manuscript is scheduled to be turned over to production. Your goal in the revision is the same as it was when you wrote the book the first time: to get your book into the hands of the sales force in time for adoptions.

REVIEWS: WHAT THEY ARE AND HOW TO WORK WITH THEM

Your acquisitions editor will take the first step in the revision process when she or he sends the latest edition of your book out for review, often with the help of a development editor or project manager. In most cases, reviewers are instructors who have used your book in the classroom, although some reviewers may never have seen it before. The opinions from these people are the best tools we have in deciding how to improve the text in the next edition. Reviews also alert us to market changes and to the strengths and weaknesses of the competition.

You can join with your editor to put together the reviewer questionnaire. Reviewers' answers to these questions, as well as their personal observations of how well the text works in the classroom, will give you a great deal to go on when you start your revision.

Your editor will glean a list of revision guidelines from the reviewers' comments and give them to you in the form of a review summary. Thus, you will see at a glance the key points you should keep in mind as you add and delete material. Your editor will also send you a full set of the actual reviews, which you should consult as you work on the text.

In most cases, we test the market once more by sending all or part of your newly revised manuscript out for review. We take this step to make sure that your manuscript changes are acceptable and attractive to the market. Although yet another round of revision may follow, remember that our ultimate goal is to improve on quality and sales in the new edition.

MORE IDEA SOURCES

Product Team: The members of your book product team, including your acquisitions editor, development editor, marketing manager, and project manager, may also give you other valuable information to use along with the reviewers' comments.

Product Information Forms: Our sales representatives are trained to ask about a book's strengths and weaknesses while instructors are using the book in the classroom and to pass these comments on to the acquisitions editor and marketing manager in the form of **Product Information Forms (PIFs)**. Your editor will keep a PIF file over the years the current edition is in use and give it to you when the revision begins.

Other Idea Sources: Occasionally, we conduct mail or phone surveys of potential users to learn more about the current market. Our sales staff may also target certain customers for in-depth interviews about your book, its competition, and the market as a whole. Once again, all of these results will be given to you before your revision work begins.

WHAT YOU CAN DO TO MAKE YOUR REVISION EASIER

Authors who have been through the revision process have found that the following techniques help make the job a lot easier.

1. Keep alert to changes in the competition by examining your competitors' revisions carefully whenever they appear. The content or pedagogical changes that your competitors make in new editions have often been recommended by users from your own book's potential audience.
2. Keep a running file of materials that might be useful in future editions of your book. Have a file folder for each of your book's chapters into which

you drop clippings from periodicals, interesting applications, handwritten reminder notes to yourself, and any other items that you think might come in handy later on. It is much better to set up and use such a system between revision-writing periods than to have to scramble for usable material at the eleventh hour.

3. Keep a special copy of your book in which you jot marginal notes and ideas for clarifying the text. These ideas may occur to you during classroom discussions, while preparing exams, when grading papers, while looking at competing texts, and so on.

By following these suggestions, you will be well prepared to start your revision on time—with minimal stress. Most important, you will be able to focus on writing new text, creating new artwork, and reorganizing the flow of ideas rather than on gathering raw material.

PREPARING THE REVISED TEXT

If you are reusing a large portion of material from the last edition and have only light to moderate changes throughout the manuscript, talk to your acquisitions editor about whether preparing a tearsheet manuscript might make for an easier production effort than getting a copy of the final disks from the previous edition. If it is decided that a **download** of the previous edition *is* preferable, specify whether you require Macintosh or IBM-compatible disks and what software program you will be using. Our prepress department will contact the vendor and will supply your editor with the disks in the format you require if at all possible. (Note that this is less likely if yours is a mathematics text.) If you are making major revisions throughout, you may wish to key the manuscript from scratch. Prepare the manuscript as you would a new manuscript. (See Chapters 6–9 for our earlier discussion on the physical preparation of text and illustrations).

REVISING THE ART MANUSCRIPT

Revised illustrations fall into five different categories. As you will see, these categories affect the way the art is handled.

PICKUP LINE ART AND PICKUP LINE ART WITH CORRECTIONS

Pickup line art can be reused from the current edition of your book or another Addison-Wesley title as is, requiring, at most, a revised figure number. In contrast, although the basic structure of **pickup line art with corrections** remains the same, minor changes are needed. You may, for example, want to change some illustration labels, update data, or correct a mistake that slipped through in the last edition.

To revise these two types of art, start by pasting up the tearsheet illustrations from the latest printing of the most recent edition. Be sure that each tearsheet shows the old figure number and the old book page number so that we can easily keep track of the illustrations. If tearsheets are not available, or if you prefer to keep the text and illustration tearsheets intact, use a photocopy of the full book page to create a separate art manuscript. If you are using illustrations from another Addison-Wesley title (whether pickup line art or pickup line art with corrections), identify the source on the art manuscript page, complete with full title, edition number, page number, and figure number.

When indicating a new figure number on pickup line art, simply mark through the old number and insert a new number above or to the left of the old number. Please do not make it impossible for us to read the old figure (or book page) number. Once again, it will make your editor's job a lot harder if old numbers are not readable.

Indicate minor corrections on the tearsheet in the same way as you see in Figure 13.1.

NEW LINE ART

In a revision, **new line art** refers to illustrations appearing in the text for the first time, or illustrations from the previous edition with major changes (if you are uncertain what constitutes a major change, consult your editor). Prepare new art for the revision following the guidelines described in Chapter 9 of this *Author's Guide*. Keep in mind that any new art you include in the revision must be consistent with the current art. The basic style, structure, and editorial thrust of the text's art program have already been set, and all new art must fit comfortably into the art program.

When your art program is complete, number new line art, pickup line art, and pickup line art with corrections in sequence to make one final illustration program.

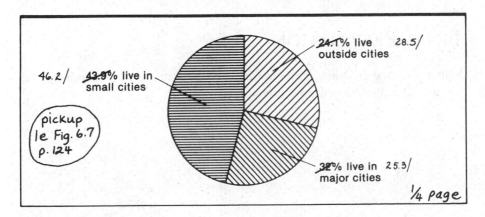

Figure 13.1 An example of pickup line art with changes marked for a revised edition.

PICKUP PHOTOS

When you use photos that appeared in the previous edition of your book or in another Addison-Wesley title, they are referred to as **pickup photos**. In preparing your pickup photo manuscript, follow the same procedures we described for pickup line art. (This category also includes pickup camera-ready art.) As a general rule, you should strive to pick up approximately 70 percent of the images from the previous edition, and replace 30 percent with new photos. Check with your editor to determine the suitability of this rule to your current revision.

NEW PHOTOS

All photos that will appear in the revised text for the first time are **new photos**. They should be prepared according to the guidelines in Chapter 9. This category also includes new camera-ready art.

REUSE AND NEW PERMISSIONS FOR TEXT AND ART

You must obtain permission for all copyrighted material in the revised text. This includes copyrighted material taken from any previous edition, as well as all new copyrighted material. Sometimes, owners of copyrighted material grant permission for use in all future editions, but you cannot count on this. On the contrary, most permissions are for one-time use only.

Your best course of action is a careful review of your permissions correspondence for each piece of copyrighted text and art. Start this process early so that you can request all your needed permissions in time. Then follow the same procedures you used for the first edition (see Chapter 5). Key all permissions letters to the manuscript, and submit them to us along with your final manuscript.

FINAL PREPARATION

Follow the same guidelines given in Chapter 6 for instructions on numbering the manuscript and shipping the manuscript to us.

Glossary

Acknowledgments Words of thanks to reviewers and others who helped develop and prepare the manuscript; following the preface. Also refers to credit to copyright holders who granted permission to use copyrighted material. These credit lines can appear with the borrowed material, on the copyright page, or at the back of the book.

Acquisitions editor Editor who signs authors to book contracts, commissions reviews, determines book length and production budget, and works with the author on manuscript development.

Annotated bibliography List of books and articles on chapter topics that includes a short description of each entry's contents.

Answer book Supplement that contains the correct answers to specified text problems not already answered in the text; common to many scientific and technical texts.

Appendix Part of back matter that contains material related to but set apart from the text.

Art editor Editor who works closely with development editor to set vision for art program and develop color palette.

Art log Record that identifies and helps keep track of all artwork; can be provided by acquisitions or development editor in electronic form or hard copy.

Art sketch Author's visual representation of an art concept, used by artist to create final art.

Assistant editor Member of editorial staff assigned to work with author during development stages of book.

Associate editor Member of editorial staff assigned to work with author during development stages of book.

Author-date references Reference system in which authors' names and publication dates are cited within the text, enclosed in parentheses. Complete bibliographical information is given at the end of each chapter or at the end of the book.

Author index Index that contains the name of all authors cited in the book.

Author queries Unresolved questions on proofs that only the author can answer.

Author's alterations (AAs) Any change in proofs other than the correction of an error introduced by the compositor.

Author's Questionnaire (AQ) Document completed by the author and used by the marketing manager to build the marketing plan for a title.

Back matter Material following the last page of the main portion of the text, such as appendixes, a glossary, reference lists, and an index.

Bibliographical essay List of books and articles on chapter topics, in which sources are discussed in narrative form.

Bibliographical notes Source citations for statements or quotations in the text, placed at the end of the chapter and numbered consecutively.

Bibliography List of all publications used to write the text, usually arranged alphabetically and placed in the back matter.

Bookseller Relations Program Program created to address specific issues brought up by bookstores.

Boxed essays (boxes) Pedagogical aids, set off from the main text, that apply academic concepts to real life or provide additional examples to clarify complex topics.

Brief table of contents List of front matter elements, part and chapter titles, and back matter elements; used in addition to a detailed table of contents.

Built-up fraction Fraction set in displayed material, for example

$$\frac{a+b}{c+d}$$

Camera-ready art Art ready to be photographed as supplied, such as printed forms, stock quotes, computer printouts, and cartoons.

Camera-ready copy Text copy such as that for supplements that is ready for printing.

Caption Brief description that accompanies illustrations. Formerly referred to as a *legend*.

Case studies Readings that apply academic concepts to real-world examples.

Chapter outline List of main chapter headings at the beginning of each chapter or part.

Complimentary copies (sample copies) Free textbooks or supplements given to instructors or adoption committee members for examination, to help make a sale.

Compositor Facility where proof stages are generated and corrected. Also called a *typesetter*.

Compositor errors (PEs) Formerly called *printer's errors*, these are mistakes made by compositor during initial keyboarding of manuscript or while making changes in proofs.

Coordinating author Author who works with editors and contributors during a book's development, writes the introduction and part openers, and acts as final arbiter in disputes about text content and style.

Copyediting Stage in production process in which the text is polished for grammar and style and is prepared for composition.

Copyeditor Editor who checks spelling, punctuation, grammar; catches any inconsistency of style and form; and marks design codes on the manuscript for compositor.

Copyright Exclusive legal right to reproduce, publish, and sell a literary, dramatic, musical, or artistic work.

Core Publishing Team Staff members who work to implement the authorial and editorial vision of the project and share responsibility for its budgetary goals. Members include the Presigning Team and a project editor, an associate or assistant editor, and a production supervisor.

Creative services manager Extended Publishing Team member who helps design and develop marketing and advertising materials.

Credit line Notation that includes the precise wording requested by the copyright holder for use of borrowed material.

Cropping A means to indicate that only a certain portion of a photo is to be used.

Custom book manager Manager who works with sales, editorial, and marketing personnel to adapt textbooks to the special needs of professors, schools, or associations.

Dedication Personal message of thanks, usually given to a special person or persons who helped the author develop the manuscript or who gave the author support during the project; appears on or following the copyright page.

Designer Graphic artist who makes decisions about the many factors that define a book's appearance, such as typefaces, chapter opener layout, and the style for tables, boxed text, and end-of-chapter material.

Development editor Editor assigned to develop books in large adoption markets.

Download Electronic files of the previous edition of a text, provided by the compositor in whatever format is required.

Editorial assistant Staff member who works with the author throughout the project, sending manuscript out for review, compiling summary information, and so forth.

Em dash Two hyphens that when typeset will appear as a long dash.

Extended Publishing Team Group that includes the Core Publishing Team plus a number of skilled specialists who offer guidance and input during the early stages of product planning and who implement all aspects of the production plan.

Extract Previously published text quotation of five or more printed lines that is set off from regular text and not enclosed in quotation marks. One line of poetry or one line from a song must be treated as an extract.

Fair use The limited use of copyrighted material without the need to obtain permission.

Font Typeface used in text and headings.

Footnote Informative note placed at the bottom of a table or page.

Footnote reference Superscript reference in a table or text to information included at the bottom of the table or page.

Front matter Material that comes before Chapter 1 or Part 1 of the text, such as the table of contents and the preface.

FTP (file transfer protocol) Method of sending files to the publisher electronically.

Glossary Definitions of key terms used in the text; usually placed in the back matter.

Half title page Page i of the text, comprising only the book's full title.

Headings Text elements used to organize the text and divide it into digestible chunks.

Illustration manuscript Manuscript that includes all technical line art, three-dimensional or shaded art, and photographs. It should be separate from the text manuscript.

Illustration proofs Photocopies of newly rendered line art for the author to check.

Index A compendium of all important ideas, people, events, and so on, with page references. It is placed in the back matter.

Instructor's manual Supplement that provides instructors with teaching suggestions and other helpful ideas.

International Publishing Group Seven regional publishing and distribution companies located in many countries to serve Addison-Wesley authors and customers.

Key terms Vocabulary of a specific academic field; often boldfaced in the text where they are introduced and defined.

Keyword First important word in an index entry, by which entries are alphabetized.

Leader In art, the line extending from a label to the appropriate part of a line illustration or photograph.

Learning objectives Pedagogical element that previews the major concepts of the chapter, presented in narrative or list form.

Line art Charts, graphs, and diagrams that are drawn by an art studio.

List Information arranged in numbered, bulleted, outline, or unnumbered form that makes it easy for students to distinguish important material.

Marginal notes Key concepts or terms that are presented in the margin of a single-column text.

Marketing manager Staff member in charge of promoting text to instructors and providing sales force with a range of marketing tools.

Marketing plan Part of the marketing manager's strategy for promoting a text.

Media/software producer Staff member who works with the Presigning Team and is responsible for the development of all digital media products to accompany texts, including videos, laser discs, and CD-ROMs.

New line art Illustrations appearing in a text for the first time, or illustrations from a previous edition with major changes.

New photos All photos that will appear in a revised text for the first time.

Numbered list Items listed in a set sequence and set off from the main text.

Numbered paragraphs Lengthy discussions that need to be numbered but are too cumbersome to set off from the main text as a numbered list.

Page proofs The first stage of composition, in which the author reviews a complete set of proofs, usually in batches.

Part opener An introduction to each part of the text, containing an outline of chapters included in the part and a brief textual introduction to the part.

Pedagogical elements Learning tools that make it easy for students to understand and apply chapter content.

Permissions Authority to reprint copyrighted material granted by copyright holders.

Permissions editor Extended Publishing Team member who helps author with the permissions process.

Pickup line art Art that can be reused from the current edition of a text or from another Addison-Wesley title.

Pickup line art with corrections Art that can be reused from the current edition of a text or another Addison-Wesley title, but with minor changes.

Pickup photos Photos that appeared in the previous edition of the text or in another Addison-Wesley title and that will be reused.

Post-publication reviews Reviews comparing a newly published text with competing texts, used in developing sales strategy.

PowerPoint slides Specialized electronic presentation supplement.

Preface Part of the front matter that summarizes what the book is about. It is an important selling and marketing tool.

Prepress/media buyer Extended Publishing Team member who collaborates with others to ensure high-quality typesetting and page design.

Presigning Team Staff members who work with author to shape product vision and to flesh out plans for overall publishing process. Members include author, acquisitions editor, development manager or editor, marketing manager, and media/software producer.

Printed endpapers Copy printed on the endsheets inside the cover of a hardcover book.

Printed inside covers Copy printed on the inside covers of a paperback book.

Product Information Forms (PIFs) Customer comments on a book's strengths and weaknesses, passed on to the editors and marketing manager by sales representatives.

Production process Stages a manuscript goes through before becoming a bound book.

Production supervisor (project editor) Editor who oversees the production process, working closely with the author and acquisitions and development editors. Keeps book on schedule and oversees the entire production cycle, including copyediting and various text and art proof stages.

Project manager Member of the editorial staff assigned to work with the author during the development stages of the book.

Proofreader Person hired to read page proof against the copyedited manuscript and to check for typographical errors.

Proofs Duplicate copies of electronically composed material and artwork; used for reviewing text and art and correcting errors before printing.

Public domain Refers to material on which copyright has expired or material that, owing to its nature, is not protected by copyright.

Quotations Material from another source used word for word. Short quotations of no more than three lines can be run in with the text and enclosed in quotation marks.

Reprint and archive coordinator Extended Publishing Team member who maintains a file of any text errors and makes sure that they are corrected when the book is reprinted.

Reprint corrections Changes made to correct mistakes in content, credits, or permissions when the book is reprinted.

Reviewing process Process of evaluating the project in stages from the initial proposal through the publication of the finished text.

Review questions Questions that generally fall at the end of each chapter and test students' knowledge of what they have read.

Reviews Opinions of academic experts on text quality; reviews are obtained at different stages in the manuscript development process and before a revision is undertaken.

Sales representative Member of the sales staff who travels throughout an assigned sales territory, visiting schools and calling regularly on instructors.

Sample problems and solutions Pedagogical aid that shows students how to approach and solve typical problems, commonly found in introductory or intermediate economics texts.

Selected bibliography Bibliography broken into sections by subject.

Sexist language Language that stereotypes male and female roles and uses male pronouns in all cases.

Solidus (fraction) Fraction set within text lines, for example, $(a + b)/(c + d)$.

Solutions manual Supplement that shows all the steps needed to work out designated text problems.

Source note Complete publication information for material being reprinted from another source.

Student solutions manual Supplement that offers solutions to odd-numbered exercises from the text.

Study guide Supplement that gives students the opportunity to review important text concepts and to apply those concepts to questions and problems.

Style sheet List of decisions on how to spell technical terms and treat capitalization, abbreviations, and so on; used to ensure consistency in the manuscript.

Subject index Index that includes proper names and subjects.

Subscripts Characters placed below the normal line of type; commonly used in mathematical and chemical equations.

Substantive footnotes Editorial comments that are necessary to the understanding of the text, placed at the bottom of a page.

Summaries Pedagogical aids that help students learn the material in a chapter by recapping and reinforcing critical concepts in narrative or list form.

Superscripts Characters placed above the normal line of type; commonly used in footnotes and mathematical and chemical equations.

Supplements Free and salable materials that are part of a text package.

Supplements editor Extended Publishing Team member who coordinates the development and production of text supplements.

Tabbing guide Marketing tool designed to "walk" a prospective customer through a book, identifying the most exciting content and pedagogical features.

Table Data presented in columns and rows to communicate difficult or complicated concepts in a shorthand way.

Table of contents Outline of part titles, chapter titles, first-level and sometimes second-level text heads and text page numbers.

Tearsheets Pages torn from a bound book.

Technical art supervisor Extended Publishing Team member who evaluates files from art vendors and/or authors and advises authors on file preparation.

Telesales representative Sales staff member who uses the telephone to make sales calls.

Test bank Supplement containing a battery of short questions and answers, produced in electronic or printed form; also known as a *test item file*.

TestGen EQ Addison-Wesley's computerized test generator, available in Windows and Macintosh versions.

Title page Front matter page that includes the book's complete main title, subtitle, edition, author's name and affiliation, and publisher's name and logo.

Transparencies Supplement consisting of line illustrations and photographs taken from the text or of supplementary key illustrative material.

Trim size Final trimmed size of the book.

Virus-protection software Software used to check computers and disks for viruses and "clean" them if necessary.

Index